Planet Forex

Abe Cofnas

Planet Forex

Currency Trading in the Digital Age

Abe Cofnas
Learn4X
Longwood, FL, USA

ISBN 978-3-319-92912-5   ISBN 978-3-319-92913-2   (eBook)
https://doi.org/10.1007/978-3-319-92913-2

Library of Congress Control Number: 2018949048

Cover image © Creative-Touch / Getty Images
Cover design by Thomas Howey

Printed on acid-free paper

This Palgrave Macmillan imprint is published by the registered company Springer International Publishing AG part of Springer Nature.
The registered company address is: Gewerbestrasse 11, 6330 Cham, Switzerland

Preface

This book is about the intersection of fundamentals, sentiment, and technical analysis in the currency markets. It is written for people who are interested in gaining an edge in forex trading. In particular, for traders who are beginning to test the waters in currency trading, it provides guidance on how to integrate fundamental knowledge to better assess price action. For the more experienced trader who has focused mainly on technical analysis, our objective is to supplement technical analysis trading with insights into which fundamental forces are impacting price movements. This book aims to assist traders to develop and apply a fundamental and sentiment mind-set to trading currency markets.

Let us think back to just before the year 2000. That was the era of dedicated phone lines and green screen monitors at brokerage firms. Markets were slow. As a result, the prevailing strategy was "buy and hold." In this era, traders were at the mercy of their brokers. Information was in asymmetrical pockets of knowledge. Then the rise of computers and the internet destroyed the old order and changed the world of trading. Today, information is now everywhere and mostly free. But the data flow is often unreliable and mixed with rumors and hyperbole. Yet trading execution is lightning fast and as a result markets move equally fast in reaction.

In today's fast-paced globalized world of information, integrating fundamental analysis with technical analysis is more important than ever before. The digital era has made trading at the same time easier, as data acquisition and trading can be done anywhere, from the beaches of Miami, to the streets of Mumbai. Smart devices enable instant trading. Yet, trading is also more complicated because markets are more complex than ever before, and more volatile as news acts as information shocks and cascades quickly through cross market asset classes. John Netto, a leading trader states:

> Globalization has created a swath of financial news sources, social media outlets, and inexpensive research available on the internet. This information has created a new balance, changing global macro investing from a long-term strategy focused on large thematic bets to being woven in the day-to-day price action of every asset class at every price level. The markets eat, breathe, and run on global macro themes … The interconnectivity of the world has melded global macro investing philosophies into all other investment philosophies to the point they are inseparable.[1]

In the age of the internet, trading experience presents many challenges to traders and one is reminded of the ancient saying in the Book of Ecclesiastes that "there is no wisdom without pain."

Currency traders experience several pain points in their journey into trading. The first is selecting the wrong pair to trade. A second pain point is putting on a trade in the wrong direction. Having targets that are based on belief rather than on evidence is a very important third pain point. Finally, after achieving a profitable trade, many traders get out too early. These pain points are very much the result of a false dichotomy that postulates there is a difference between fundamental and technical analysis, or that all one needs is technical analysis to trade currency markets.

A goal of this book is also to provide forex traders with what they need to know to reduce the time it takes to become good enough at forex training to treat it as a profession. Malcom Gladwell famously referred to 10,000 hours as the amount of time necessary to become an expert. In chess, Garry Kasparov has referenced 10,000 patterns or 50,000 positions. For forex traders, this book on trading fundamentals and sentiment patterns will hopefully build the skills for successful trading in far less time.

---

[1] The Global Macro Edge, The Pelican Trader, 2016 John Netto, Page 13.

Ultimately, a successful trader is one who is not only profitable, but is able to adapt to a changing global landscape. In today's digital trading environment, the attributes of trader fitness must include an understanding of fundamental forces, sentiment patterns, and technical analysis.

FL, USA   Abe Cofnas

Contents

List of Charts

List of Tables

1

What is Fundamental Analysis?

Fundamental analysis, or a fundamental view of currency markets, is widely misunderstood. It is not simply about the economic conditions facing a country. Fundamental analysis, when properly understood, contains sentiment analysis. Let us state this another way. Fundamental analysis deals with economic forecasts and expectations about economic metrics such as CPI (consumer price index), GDP (gross domestic product), employment, and so on. These fundamental expectations involve longer- and medium-term durations. The exact mix of expectation durations is, in fact, always changing. Sometimes expectations of economic outcomes a year ahead may impact current price action. At other times, the immediate geopolitical and global economic conditions have an immediate impact.

In a way, this view of a fundamental structure behind currency movements is similar to recent discoveries in physics of the Higgs boson field. In that major discovery, it has been proven that electrons get their mass as they go through the Higgs boson field. In currency trading we can say that prices get their direction and strength of direction as they go through a field filled with fundamental expectation forces. Sentiment is the bridge and transmission channel, between long-term and short-term economic expectations that directly act upon the price.

Within the rubric of fundamental analysis, sentiment analysis focuses on current expectations about whether prior fundamental forecasts are correct. In other words, sentiment is the measure of the immediate change in expectations, caused by data releases, geopolitical crises, or any other information shock that reaches the markets. Sentiment is about *both* long-term and short-term expectations. Sentiment is how the market expresses emotions. Emotions are always about something and in currency markets emotions are generally about risk and uncertainty. Traders, therefore, need to diagnose what the market movements are about. This contrasts greatly with the current, dominant technical view of markets and currency pairs.

What is a Currency Pair Price? A Fundamental View

An exclusive technical analysis view of markets, and in particular currency pairs, is highly flawed. The weaknesses and limits of technical analysis starts with a misunderstanding of what currency prices are all about. The currency pair is, from a technical analysis view of market reality, a point on the X–Y price axis. Charts visualize the price behavior. For example, if the EURUSD has moved 20 pips, from 1.1700 to 1.1720, a line chart will show how this movement has occurred. Candlestick charts show open, high, low, and close prices per unit of time (minute, hour, or other time slices). The X axis represents time. Simple enough. But is that what a price really is? The fact is that it is more than a measure on a X–Y axis.

The fundamental viewpoint asserts that a currency price and its accompanying charts, are *codes* that are really enciphered signatures of expectations. A better understanding of how to unlock the codes within each currency pair will enable traders to profitably ride the expectation waves that move currency prices.

Flaws in Technical Analysis

The question arises: If technical analysis has these flaws, why is it so dominant? The answer is rather simple. The dominance of technical analysis as a tool for traders is not because technical analysis is totally effective, but because *it is easy to sell systems* and courses offering hyperbolic performance promises. It is natural that traders want to find the holy grail for predicting direction. As a result, responding to the desires and hopes of traders, there is extensive marketing of signals and systems, and courses that teach set-ups to respond to this demand. Some systems and signals are profitable. None are profitable all of the time. The products of the trading industry are designed to be produced with minimal viability, because speed to the market is a more important priority than performance effectiveness. As a result, a total reliance on technical set-ups presents many flaws. Let us explore further some of the deep flaws in using technical analysis.

The first deep flaw in exclusive reliance on technical analysis is psychological and philosophical. The very premise that one can predict that a price will reach a target is fraught with problems. The price target is in reality not technical in nature. It is a fabricated human construction. It is as subjective as searching for and finding a face in the clouds. If you look for one you will find it, but it is delusional to believe that the face in the clouds really exists. Similarly, a profit target is a point of hope in the price arena. But in trading, "hopium" is not a useful drug.

The very act of thinking that there is a target inherent in the currency pair price or pattern is also teleological (defined as inferring something has an intention). Inferring intention is a common attribute of human behavior because it is more comforting to deal with an assumed intention then to deal with uncertainty. Consider the following statements: "The price wants to go to the next Fibonacci level". "The price will bounce off resistance and then move to support". "The price will break the outer trend line and then move to the inner trend line." These types of comments are heard every day by traders and reflect the flaw that is inherent in teleological thinking in trading.

The fact is that a price does not know where it wants to go, because the price is really an instant in time of a balance between bullish and bearish expectations. A target also has the effect of suppressing profitability. Many traders who put on a trade that reaches a target price often take profit at that target, only to learn that the profits would have been higher. Technical profit targets are best used as guides only.

A second powerful source of error and weakness in trading analysis is the use and analysis of trend lines. An uptrend is technically defined as when a price has a higher high and a higher low. A downtrend, conversely is defined as when a price has a lower high and a lower low. A popular saying is: "the trend is your friend." Going with the trend seems like a good approach. But keep in mind that the trend is your friend until it is at an end. Trend analysis offers a great deal of ambiguity in detecting a shift in the trend. When is it really over? Is it at a break of a line? How thick is the line? Is it 10 pips? This difficulty of defining a break in the trend applies to both intraday and longer durations.Central banks have a very hard time pinpointing just when a break in inflation trends is occurring. That is why they notoriously act too late and allow inflation to go too far, or too early, and put breaks on growth, stimulating a recession. Precision of projecting where prices are going is a common challenge to both traders and policy markets.

Of course, lines do not exist and are just heuristic devices, which is a method to get a sense of the boundaries of price action. Lines are mathematical inventions to overlay on what we see. At best, a trend is a map of a path of prices. It leaves a great deal of room for error. It is a very low-resolution map.

Resistance and Support Lines

The concepts of resistance and support are part of the foundations of technical analysis. Like trend lines, resistance and support convey assumptions about price patterns that are ambiguous. Just when is resistance or support broken? When is resistance and support simply being probed? Current technical analysis of resistance and support treat those concepts as firm and quantifiable. They are not. We can see the inherent ambiguity in finding resistance and support (Chart 1.1).

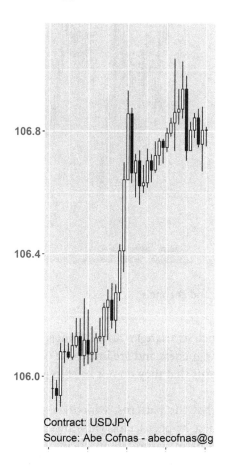

Chart 1.1   Resistance and support is hard to locate

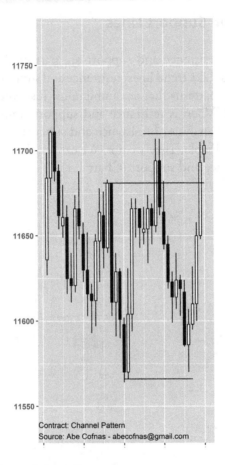

Chart 1.2 Triangles, and channels

Price patterns such as triangles and channels are patterns that exhibit similar degrees of vagueness and are imprecise when the trader attributes powers to the patterns that they do not have to predict future price direction (Chart 1.2).

Keep in mind that the patterns, which are perceived by traders, are subjective and at best ex-post facto. They are easy to see after they have formed. True patterns in nature are mathematical and can be tested by scientific methods. More importantly, they are intersubjective, which means that other people can confirm them. Price patterns are flawed because they are best-case interpretations. However, patterns do provide evidence of the status of emotions in the market.

Fibonacci levels are among the most popular tools for trading and do give insight into the nature of price action. Although the field of technical analysis ascribes nearly magical powers to Fibonacci levels, they are still not reflective of any inherent direction. When prices seem to move in Fibonacci retracement ratios it is because that is the way energy moves everywhere (the famous Nautilus shell is a classic illustration of Fibonacci patterns, and the proportions of the human face follow Fibonacci ratios), but this does not mean that they predict where the price is going. Furthermore, markets recognize where the Fibonacci points are and use them to create trading triggers. This creates a self-fulfilling process. Fib lines need to be seen as providing zones of possible resistance and support. The most important weakness in applying Fibonacci analysis relates to the confusion of where to locate a bounce or break off a fib line. This kind of thinking creates a lot of room for error. Just when can a break of a Fibonacci line be considered a break? A break is a very subjective concept. Do we consider a break when the price reaches above or below a Fib line? Or do we have to wait for a candle to close more than once above such a line? The answer may vary among different traders (Chart 1.3).

Chart wave analysis (Elliott Wave) is another popular form of technical/teleological analysis that offers traders the promise of finding and riding a direction more accurately. The problem with wave analysis is that it is not falsifiable. Prices are defined as being in waves that are part of an impulse or a corrective sequence. Within each sequence there are mini waves as well. Those who follow wave analysis find comfort in this detailed set-up, *until* prices do not follow the wave prediction. Rather than accepting the fact of being wrong, wave analysts will say that the price is correcting and then will resume back in the right direction. Many traders have heard the statement: the price will go down and then go up. *This is nonsense.* It is subjective and vague. It is misleading to the trader who wants to use a method that is reliable. When is a wave based trade wrong? Wave trading is a form of forecasting that has huge degrees of ambiguity. Riding the wave is easy when one is looking in the rear-view mirror.

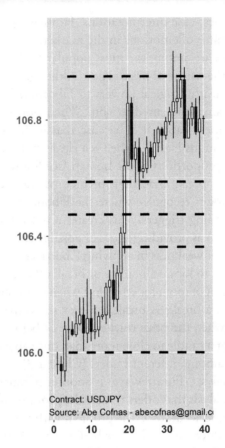

Chart 1.3 Vague bounce and breaks around Fibonacci levels

The body of technical analysis also includes popular tools such as indicators and moving averages. They have a major weakness in common: they are lagging indicators. The mathematics of their construction calculates past prices and transforms them using a variety of equations into an indicator number. They should be seen as training wheels for the new trader. As the trader gets more experienced, these wheels are taken off and the trader focuses on the price action itself. Instead, bad habits are hard to change and traders find themselves loading a chart with so many indicators that it looks like a Jackson Pollock painting! (Chart 1.4).

Chart 1.4 Jackson Pollock-inspired chart

For the new trader, trade set-ups are a common way of starting to trade currencies (Chart 1.5). They typically offer a combination of different indicators. Bollinger Bands, Fibonacci lines, and moving averages, are very popular set-ups for new traders. They do have a use as they provide an initial framework for finding a trade signal. They promote, however, a key embedded weakness, which is ignoring the price action! The trader focuses on the set-up which has a counterproductive impact; the signal gets obscured.

All forms of current technical analysis have in common the problem of egocentric myopia. Technical traders act as if the spot forex charts is all they have, and indeed all they need to be a profitable trader. The belief system of the technical trader is that prices sufficiently and fairly reflect anything the trader needs to know about the outside world. When technical analysis is exclusively relied upon, there is a likely failure of perception. Seeing a chart is not the same as perceiving the forces that are impacting the prices.

Of course, there is no perfect way to trade markets and currencies, but some mind-sets undermine the trader right from the start. Traders, especially beginners, who spend thousands of dollars on courses that have no real foundations of validity and are sold with hyperbolic promises, are prone to counterproductive behaviors. Having invested thousands of dollars, there is a natural bias toward believing in what was invested. For example, traders keep watching the charts, looking for a technical angle that will be the winning trading signal and a ride to profitability. The fact is that a chart maps current prices and previous movements. They do not reveal what caused the movement!

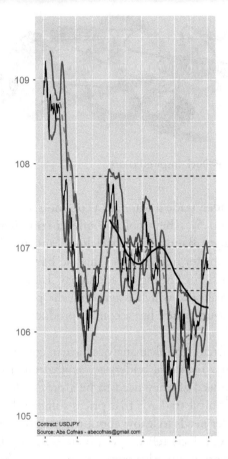

Chart 1.5   Trade set-ups generate low signal/noise

Ultimately, as traders become more experienced, they lose indicators and previous set-ups and focus on trying to understand why a price reached a certain point. The answer lies in understanding the fundamental forces that permeate the markets and diagnosing price action not as something that has a goal but is a signature of emotions. It is worthwhile to build a knowledge base of how emotions and markets and, in particular, currency pairs intertwine.

There is one more critical flaw in emphasizing technical analysis that needs to be raised: it ignores the human condition. Traders are told to eliminate emotion from trading. They are taught instead to rely on a set of rules and set-ups. But emotional intelligence is exactly what a successful trader needs to develop and apply. Learning a set-up and a trading technique is relatively easy. But learning how to deal with surprises in price action or a sequence of losses is a key survival skill that technical analysis completely ignores. A trader that is experiencing acute stress, resulting from a persistent and lingering memory of a loss, is in fact in danger of further losses until the cycle of depression is broken by a big win. Perhaps the American Psychiatric Association should amend its latest Diagnostic and Statistical Manual of Mental Disorders (DSM-5) and investigate "Trader-related disorders!" Until then, traders should pay constant attention to their emotional state and, importantly, to the emotional state of the market.

2

Core Fundamental Forces and How to Monitor Them

Let us clarify the contrast between technical and fundamental analysis. Technical analysis is static, and focuses on mapping price action. All the resulting analysis exists in a two-dimensional space along an X axis of time, and a Y axis of price. Technical traders are therefore chartists. They are the equivalent of radiologists who diagnose the structure of the body and detect patterns that point to disease or a breakdown. In contrast, fundamental traders are, in a sense, psychiatrists, and perhaps cosmologists; they diagnose the causation and the forces behind price behavior. Of course, the fundamental forces are inter-market and outside of the two dimensions of a price chart. In a sense, fundamental forces are the third dimension that deserve trader attention in trading currency pairs. While we cannot see fundamental forces, like gravity and electricity, we know they exist and shape our world.

Fundamental forces are also analogous to the seasons of the weather. Weather is caused by several factors, such as the spin of the Earth, the Moon and tides, uneven heating of the planet, and interaction of different atmospheric pressures. The results are experienced as weather. It is a very dynamic process. Deep in winter, a warm day can occur, but it is an outlier event. It can snow in July in Disney World in Orlando, but do not bet on it (the last time it snowed in Disney World was in 2009). Fundamental forces are the

© The Author(s) 2018
A. Cofnas, *Planet Forex*, https://doi.org/10.1007/978-3-319-92913-2_2

weather on Planet Forex! In another, deeper sense, forex prediction is similar to weather prediction. Take the case of forecasts on hurricanes. Science has not been able to precisely predict when a hurricane will form. It can detect a hurricane pattern, however, once it is formed, and then estimate a probable path. The limiting factor in weather prediction is known as the Lorenz Butterfly. Basically, the concept states that if you miss the flapping of a butterfly's wing in your calculations, you will have an error in the forecast that can lead to a large error in accuracy. This phenomenon points to the condition known as *irreducible complexity*. When applied to forex trading, we simply do not know all of the variables that impact the price action, and therefore forecasting price direction is subject to great deal of error. Yet, we can reduce the uncertainty by understanding the core fundamental forces.

The Set of Core Fundamental Forces

How shall we think about fundamentals from the perspective of using fundamentals for trading forex? Let us get right to it. There are many variables that can be considered to be part of fundamentals. Almost too many to count. Which fundamental forces should be detected, and which could be ignored? The answer is simple: The most important fundamental forces for traders are those that result in a shift in bullish or bearish expectations. Let us categorize the different bullish and bearish forces.

Forces of Growth

Growth in an economy is an important bullish force. Anything that contributes to the expectations of continued growth acts to strengthen a currency because a stronger economy attracts capital from outside to buy the exported products of that economy. Expectations of a stronger economy also encourages consumer spending. Expectations of growth spurs increased employment. In Planet Forex, using our weather metaphor, economies grow and become perhaps over-heated, or slow down and cool. Oh yes, sometimes there are catastrophic storms and shocks.

Forces of Decline

An economy slowing down, or expected to slow down, generates a bearish force. When unemployment increases, when inflation gets high, there is a slowdown in actual or projected spending. Some bearish forces are very latent. For example, the aging of the population generates a future slowdown in spending. Japan faces this problem more than any other country. But demographic forces are very slow moving. Additionally, technological innovation is a major deflationary force as it suppresses prices. Tomorrow's big flat-screen television will be much less costly than today's. Why not wait to buy it next year? Disruptive technologies and companies such as Amazon and Uber have great success while undermining established sectors. The result is economic uncertainy generating market anxiety.

Expectations on Interest Rate Direction

Virtually anything that contributes to expectations of the economic weather changing becomes important because this leads to expectations about interest rate changes. Changes in labor market conditions, including employment, wage price growth, consumer spending, saving rates, and inflation, are force factors that directly strength or weaken bullish or bearish expectations. But to shape our trades we have to get more granular. We have to ask: expectations about what? It is mostly expectations about whether the central banks will increase, decrease, or continue monetary policies. Since the key tool used by central banks is adjusting interest rates, trading fundamentals becomes trading expectations on interest rate changes! All currency prices ultimately reflect expectations about the direction of interest rates.

Forces of Fear

Fear of trade wars, asset bubbles, market corrections, crashes, terrorism, and global slowdowns, all comprise a set of fears that push and pull as fundamental forces on the currency pairs. They are important because they impact the day-to-day, and sometimes, hour-by-hour, market emotions. The trader is advised to be aware of which fears are dominating the news.

It is also important to discern which currencies may gain or lose strength in response to the fears. For example, the Canadian, Australian, and Mexican currencies will be sensitive to fears of trade wars. Of course, the US Dollar will be a focus of such fears as well.

How Market Patterns Emerge

To reinforce a shift in mind-set from an exclusive technical analysis view to a fundamental analysis perspective, another way to understand why and how fundamental forces impact market prices is to visualize the market (set of all prices) as a swarm that shifts shape and direction when there is a catalyst/stimulus that probes the boundaries of the swarm. A single ant or bee is not very smart, but their colony's behavior emerges as having a nonrandom shape. Watch a school of fish, a flock of birds, or a swarm of bees. Watch how they instantly move and shift shape and form a collective direction. It looks organized. It looks like the direction and forward movement is designed and intentional, but there is no organizer. Similarly, our markets swarm and react to many different variables. The price direction can shift quickly, but there is a discernable pattern. Even if the trader does not know what is moving the markets, the shape of the price patterns reveal that something has happened. By looking at the market as being like a swarm the trader can apply strategies and analytics that detect trades that ride that swarm! Based on this underlying feature of swarm behavior, swarm intelligence programs are now emerging that model markets based on equations that model swarm behavior. One such new AI trading program, called Enigma Signal (www.enigmasignal.com), applies these concepts to forex trading (see Chap. 8). A recent example of a "currency" that can be best understood as reflecting swarm behavior is bitcoin (Chart 2.1). Crypto currency buyers are buying because others are buying and vice versa for sellers. In a similar way, the spread of the influenza virus into a pandemic reflects the same crowd behavior pattern where contagion works in waves. Contagion of a virus assumes a parabolic path until it reaches a peak. These contagion patterns are very similar to market patterns in response to a shock. The take-away for the trader is that the price is not two dimensional, but very much a crowd/swarm behavioral phenomenon. This is a critical knowledge.

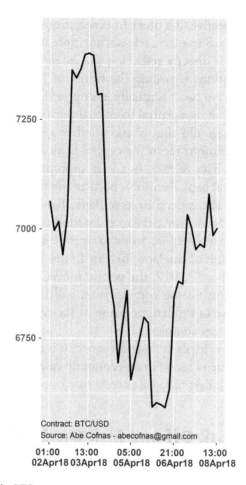

Chart 2.1   Bitcoin BTC

Source: *Harvard Business Review*, May 2001.
"Swarm Intelligence, A Whole New Way to Think About Business."
Eric Bonabeau and Christopher Meyer.

Filtering the Signal from the Noise

While the potential number of fundamental variables is enormous, the trader is challenged to filter the signal from the noise. The signal, from a fundamental perspective, is a break in expectations. This brings us to the role of data releases. Some data releases are more important than others. Their importance is directly reflecting the extent that they impact the balance of expectations regarding the future of monetary and interest rate policies. A Trump tweet is usually less impactful on a currency price, compared to a speech by a central bank chairperson. In looking at a data release, the trader should simply ask whether a surprise in the release would affect expectations regarding central bank actions. One need not be glued to every data release. But it is appropriate for the trader to closely watch central bank decisions, particularly those of the major central banks, such as the Federal Reserve Bank, Bank of England, and the European Central Bank. Since the recent period of quantitative easing is essentially over, the markets are prone to surprise at a central bank's decision. When the Bank of England increased rates for the first time since Brexit, on November 2, 2017, the pound moved over 230 pips (Chart 2.2). The uncertainty in the coming years will be whether the central banks will continue to tighten, or pause as the recovery from the great 2008 collapse becomes complete.

So, one of the key rituals of traders, every day, is to check the Economic calendar. A convenient access to an economic calendar is the site: www. forexfactory.com Traders have easy access to economic calendars.

Measuring Risk-Off and Risk-On Conditions

In addition to scanning the economic calendar, the trader should take a quick overview of market conditions. This is also known as "Regime Conditions," which is defined by trader Jason Roney as "the total market environment encapsulating all pertinent fundamental, technical, and sentiment data for a particular asset class" (*The Global Macro Edge*, p. 57).[1] Recognizing that for the human trader measuring the total market environment is virtually impossible due to its irreducible complexity, the forex trader can achieve a reliable measure of market conditions by focusing on whether the markets are risk-on or risk-off.

---

[1] John Netto, 2017. *The Global Macro Edge*, p. 57.

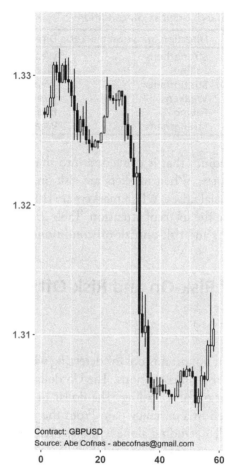

Chart 2.2   Nov 2, 2017 Bank of England raises rates for first time since Brexit!

Envision a conversation between two traders named Joe and Bob. Joe, says "How are you trading the US dollar today?" Bob replies: "It looks like the markets are risk-on and therefore I am looking for buying signals." In a real sense, all directional decisions on trading currencies imply a conclusion on whether the markets are risk-on or risk-off.

After all is said and done, equity markets provide evidence of optimism or pessimism on the economic prospects facing a country. Currencies

Table 2.1 Markets and risk-on/risk-off conditions

Underlying asset	Direction in risk-on markets	Direction in risk-off markets
US dollar	Strengthens	Weakens
VIX	Falling	Rising
Yen/dollar (JPY/USD)	Strengthens	Weakens
Gold	Weakens	Strengthens
Bond yields	Falling	Rising
Crude oil	Strengthens	Weakens

simply are the medium that is converted into shares, bonds, commodities, and other assets. When markets are risk-on, there is little fear of economic or financial crises. When markets are risk-off, fear of economic difficulties become the focus of attention. Table 2.1 shows the basic relationship of markets and risk-on/risk-off conditions.

Summary of Risk-On and Risk-Off Conditions

US dollar

The US dollar is an important tool for detecting whether the overall market has risk-on or risk-off conditions. The US dollar, however, is a misnomer in the context of forex trading. The dollar in one's wallet is not the dollar that is traded in a currency pair. From the perspective of a trader, there is no US dollar standing alone without a reference to other currencies. There are, however, three types of US dollar indexes. They are USDX, DXY, and Trade Weighted Indexes. Forex traders use mostly the USDX (Chart 2.3).

Trade weighted indexes also present evidence of currency strength as they reflect the trading relationship of the US with other countries. The trade weighted index is used by central banks to assess whether a currency is getting too strong or too weak in the context of global trade. For the spot forex trader, the USDX is the most commonly used index to monitor and trade.

The USDX provides an easy gauge to track whether the markets are experiencing positive or negative emotions. If the US dollar strengthens, then money flows to US assets. If the US dollar weakens, money goes to

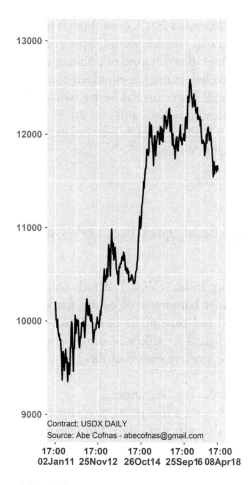

Chart 2.3 The US dollar index

the sidelines until the fear is over. When focusing on the Eurozone, or Nikkei, or other stock markets associated with a currency, a similar relationship between the equity market and the currency of that country occurs. When a currency weakens, it means that the exports of that country will be more competitive. Export sectors will tend to increase. If a currency strengthens, it reduces the profitability of that export sector and the equities associated with that sector decline in value. With regard to the USDX, at first glance, it declined in price after the Federal Reserve raised the rates in December 2017, even though rates and expectation of rates rose. Conventional wisdom would expect the currency to strength alongside rate increases. But this kind of thinking is only partially correct. The price also has to reflect market emotions about the world economy and geopolitical crises. The result has been a weaker dollar than expected during the rise in rates from 2017 and into 2018. The trader should keep in mind that the US Dollar moves in reaction to multiple forces and it is not two-dimensional in nature.

VIX

Here is the Chicago Board Option Exchange's (CBOE) description of the VIX:

The CBOE Volatility Index® (VIX® Index) is considered by many to be the world's premier barometer of equity market volatility. The VIX Index is based on real-time prices of options on the S&P 500® Index (SPX) and is designed to reflect investors' consensus view of future (30-day) expected stock market volatility.[2]

The VIX is known as the "fear index."

When it moves toward a low point near support it indicates that the markets are calm and in a buying mode. But when it moves higher toward probing its recent highs and breaking through them, the markets are facing uncertainty and assets are being liquidated into cash. A good example is the week of February 5 and 9, 2018 when the Dow, on Monday February 5, had a range of 1597 points, with a high of 25,520 and a low of 23,923.

Only to be followed on February 9 with the Dow Jones Industrial Index falling from a high of 24, 382 to a low of 23,360 (1022 points). During that week the VIX surged in volatility by 25%. Fear took over (Chart 2.4).

---

[2] www.CBOE.COM

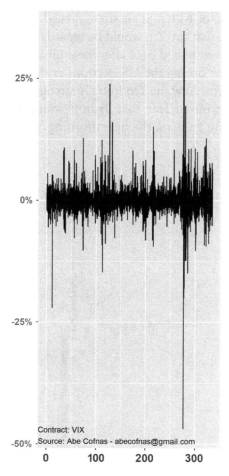

25%

0%

-25%

Contract: VIX
-50% .Source: Abe Cofnas - abecofnas@gmail.com
0   100   200   300

Chart 2.4   VIX volatility

The Yen Strengthening

In risk-off conditions, where the market desires to seek a safe haven, the Yen gets stronger. This phenomenon is not thoroughly understood, but it is a reliable pattern when there is increasing fear in the market. The fear could be due to geopolitical crises or a major disaster, such as the Fukishma earthquake of March 11, 2011. When the Earthquake occurred the reaction of fear caused the Yen to strengthen against the US dollar by the enormous amount of 611 pips. It strengthened as market expectations were initially such that the Yen would be repatriated back into the country. The Yen however, pulled back after these initial fears abated. The Yen also reacted to fears during the US elections as shown in Chart 2.5. The chart below confirms how the Yen initially strengthened during US election night in the initial fear that Trump would win. This is classic crowd behavior. By 1:00 am the next morning, the fear was over when

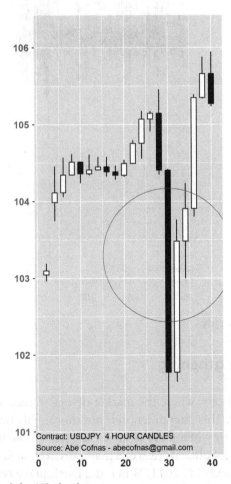

Contract: USDJPY 4 HOUR CANDLES
Source: Abe Cofnas - abecofnas@gmail.com

Chart 2.5 Yen and the US elections

Trump was the apparent winner. The Yen acted on US election night as a gauge of sentiment.

Gold is historically an asset class where it rises in price when there is fear in the market in response to a geopolitical crisis. Sudden event catalysts for gold prices rising generate parabolic moves that can be seen as temporary in nature. Gold usually works in the opposite direction to the US dollar. Not surprisingly, coinciding with the financial crisis, gold had one of its biggest upward moves in history on Sept 16, 2008. It had an opening price of 779.75 and closed at 863.85 (Chart 2.6). This is an increase of over 10% in one day. Such a move was a clear omen of the magnitude of the impending and long duration of the financial crises.

Bonds: The Market's Vigilantes

When markets experience anxiety about conditions, money seeks safer assets. Government Bonds fulfill the role of providing a relatively safe place for capital. Bond markets are often overlooked by forex traders because of the mind-set that currency price charts are sufficient to understand and predict direction. However, a great deal of insight into market expectations on currencies can be gained by following bond markets. The bond market is known to provide a gauge of macro attitudes on the risk environment regarding a country, known as "bond vigilantes." Consider the fact that the 10-year US bond yield on September 30, 1981 reached 15.8%. A clear warning of a very risk-off environment was developing. On December 22, 2017, as the year ended the yield on the 10-year bond reached a 2.54%. Traders will note that when the 10-year US note yield probes or surpasses 3%, a great deal of attention will be generated on the Bond market as a potential omen of the beginnings of a risk-off market.

It is also particularly relevant to measure the yields and perceived relative risk of the 10-year bond of different countries. For example, the 10-year government bond of Germany offers a much lower yield than the 10-year government bond of Spain. It is because the markets require higher yields to compensate for the greater perceived risk of Spain. Underscoring the importance that bond patterns are harbingers of economic changes, the *Financial Times*, December 11, 2017 reviewed the China markets and led with a headline: "China volatility clouds Investment Outlook. Sell-off

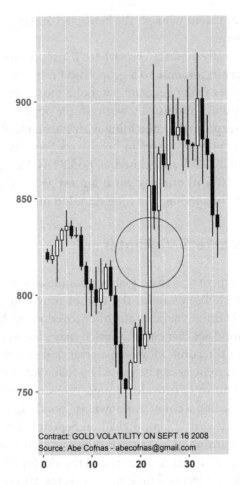

Chart 2.6 Gold and crises

prompts fears of impending slowdown as government bond yields jumped."
Evidently, the Bond Vigilantes are a global phenomenon!

The trader should look carefully as to whether the US 10-year bond
yield is increasing compared to other countries. This is important because
capital will tend to flow to the US dollar and strengthen it as a place of
greater return. An easy source for finding the different yields among key
countries is the *Financial Times* (Table 2.2). In scanning the comparative
yields, we can see a striking difference between the 10-year US Treasury

Table 2.2 Comparative 10-year bond yields on January 1, 2018

Interest rates	Yield
US Government 10-year	2.43
UK Government 10-year	1.23
German Government 10-year	0.43
Japan Government 10-year	0.05
US Government 30-year	2.76

Source: Financial Times

yield of 2.49% and the Japanese Government 10-year yield of 0.05%. In this observation, the question arises of why the Japanese 10-year yield remains close to 0%? The forex trader should know the answer. The short answer is that the Bank of Japan was forcing the 10-year note to be zero to encourage spending as part of its stimulation policy called QQE (Quantitative and Qualitative Easing).

Bond Market Shows Inflation Expectations

A quick check on whether inflation expectations are increasing can be gained by looking at an Exchange Traded Fund (ETF) that tracks these expectations as expressed in the bond market. ProShares Inflation Expectations ETF (Symbol Rinf.k) (Chart 2.7). The chart indicates the upward direction of the share price of this ETF. By the end of 2017, inflation expectations were clearly going up and in sync with Federal Reserve projections. Let us take a closer look at how inflation expectations are generated.

TIPS

TIPS are a key factor in the inflation expectation equation. Here is what the US Treasury says about TIPS:

> Treasury Inflation-Protected Securities, or TIPS, provide protection against inflation. The principal of a TIPS increases with inflation and decreases with deflation, as measured by the Consumer Price Index. When a TIPS matures, you are paid the adjusted principal or original principal, whichever is greater. TIPS are issued in terms of 5, 10, and 30 years.

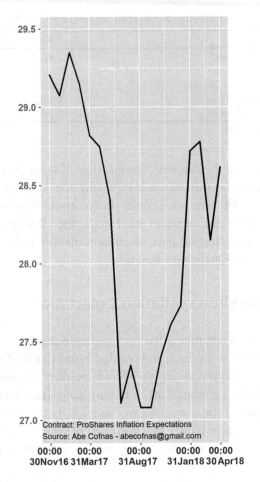

Chart 2.7 Inflation expectations shown in ETF

The key idea behind tracking inflation expectations is to understand that a Treasury Yield is composed of the TIPS yield + Expected Inflation. So by tracking the difference between the TIPS and the Treasury Yield we are able to track inflation expectations (Table 2.3). If the spreads narrow towards 0 and in fact became negative, we have conditions known as a flattening yield curve.

As mentioned earlier, the forex trader does not have to worry about what to follow, the ETF does the job for us. Still, let us be sure that one understands why this is important to the forex trader? The reason is that

Table 2.3 The US dollar index

10-year vs 2-year yield	58.6
30-year vs 5-year yield	58.1

Source: Thompson Reuters

a rising expectation in inflation will create bullish pressures on the US dollar and vice versa. There are similar ETFs that track inflation expectations for other countries.

Flattening and Inverse Yield Curve

Let us look at the famous concept of the flattening yield curve. It is very well known as a leading indicator of a slowdown in the economy. This is when the difference between a 10-year and 2-year Treasury yield is narrowing (or the 30-year and 5-year curve (Table 2.3)). The short-term yield rises when the central bank seeks to raise rates. But the longer-term yield does not go up if expectations of longer-term inflation and less long-term growth are also occurring.

On December 24, 2017, these two comparisons were calculated by Reuters:

Here is what the president of the Minneapolis Federal Reserve described in relation to the yield curve at the end of 2017:

> I believe the FOMC's rate increases are directly affecting the yield curve: As the FOMC has raised rates, the front end of the curve is moving up with our policy moves, which is to be expected. But because the Committee has been raising rates in a low inflation environment, we are sending a hawkish signal, which is likely holding down the long end of the curve by depressing inflation expectations. (https://mail.google.com/mail/u/0/#inbox/160 6f96fc32f73340)

An inverted yield curve, where short rates are above long rates, is one of the best signals we have of elevated recession risk and has preceded every single recession in the past 50 years. If the yield curve inverts it is an accepted sign of a potential recession. FX Traders should watch it. This can be done at: https://frcd.stlouisfed.org/series/T10Y2Y. A very useful further explanation of the concept behind an inverted yield curve can be found in the following New York Times article: What's the Yield Curve? 'A Powerful Signal of Recessions' Has Wall Street's Attention By Matt Phillips June 25, 2018.

The Commodity Complex; Crude and Copper

Crude oil reflects longer-term optimism or pessimism regarding global growth. Although there has been an emergence of "green" technologies, the world still runs on crude oil. Crude oil prices at the end of 2017 began

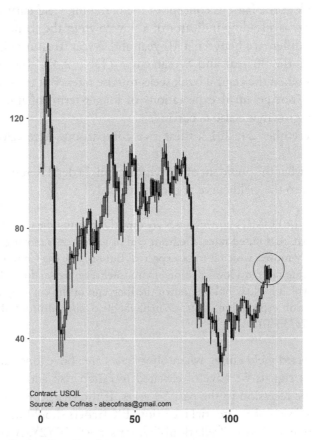

Chart 2.8   Crude oil on the rise

to probe the $60s far from the deep lows at $25 of Jan 2016. Keep in mind the that oil in the $60 (as of April 2018 (see the circle in Chart 2.9)) is far from the $140 price in July 2018 (Chart 2.8). A sharp increase in crude oil is often in response to geopolitical crises or supply disruptions. Crude price is often a gauge of expectations regarding OPEC's (Organization of the Petroleum Exporting Countries) capabilities of limiting production. The fracking technology revolution has greatly limited OPEC's ability to limit supplies. The effect is more of a range of behavior in oil.

Because Canada is a net exporter of Tar Sands Oil, the Canadian dollar is impacted by crude oil news. If oil prices are increasing, the demand for

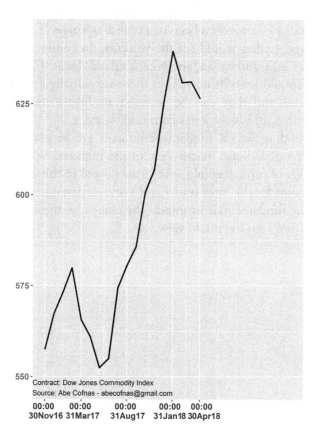

Chart 2.9   Dow Jones Commodity Price Index

Canadian dollars will increase and this is a bullish condition. The forex trader should be aware of oil supply data releases and check it on their economic calendar.

Do not forget copper. Copper is the industrial infrastructure metal that a growing economy requires. It is logical, therefore, that the demand for copper will reflect the expectations of global economic conditions and, in particular, China's growth expectations. Since Australia is a major exporter of copper, the Australian currency is the one to watch for changes in the global demand of copper.

One does not have to search far and wide to get a sense of the commodity markets. The Dow Jones Commodity Price Index is a useful overall gauge of the commodity complex including oil. We can see that the commodity complex has been in a bullish upsurge. If a sell-off occurs in this gauge, traders would see the weakness in commodity currencies such as the CAD, Australian, and New Zealand dollar (Chart 2.9).

Traders should keep in mind that there are actually a variety of Dow Jones Indexes and they can be accessed at: https://us.spindices.com/indices/commodities/dow-jones-commodity-index

Understanding which fundamental forces are in play provides the trader with a global and macro view of the markets. While there are a huge number of fundamental factors, those listed in this chapter provide a starting point for the forex trader and a foundational step towards trading with the fundamentals in mind. The challenge ahead is to translate the macro view into the micro view.

3

Understanding Central Banks and their Role in Moving Currency Markets

Having covered the key fundamental areas of market forces and conditions, the next step in trading fundamentals is gaining an understanding of the key role that central banks have on currency markets.

The elephant in the forex trading room is the central bank of a country. What central banks do is design and implement monetary policy. Their instruments of monetary policy are mainly expanding or contracting the supply of money, and varying the level of interest rates. There is controversy as to whether the central banks should have explicit rules for shifting monetary and interest rate policies, or whether policy should be situational. Whether one agrees with this mode of policy making is irrelevant, at least from the perspective of the trader. Whether one believes that the central banks are politically motivated or manipulated is also irrelevant. *What is more important is to understand that every moment in time, expectations about changes in central bank intentions for stimulus, or contraction will impact price direction.* The market, in a real sense, is a crowd of traders always sensing a potential shift in expectations about the central banks' near-term actions. Therefore, forex traders who want an edge in identifying currency direction are advised to gain a better understanding of central bank policies and behaviors. Ironically, even though central bank decisions are so important, few traders actually bother to

© The Author(s) 2018
A. Cofnas, *Planet Forex*, https://doi.org/10.1007/978-3-319-92913-2_3

read central bank statements. This is unfortunate as the central bank statements, and changes in those statements, are our modern versions of "tea leaves," and provide powerful leading indicators for predicting the direction of a currency pair.

Stimulate or Tighten: The Policy Choices of Central Banks

Let us begin by asking when and why would a currency strengthen? The direction of currencies does not occur by accident. It has a lot to do with central bank actions and policies. There are two major causes of an increase in the attractiveness of a currency. First, a currency will strengthen when there are expectations that the demand for that currency will increase. For example, if the global economy is growing and needs more crude oil, exporters of crude oil, such as Canada, will experience a greater demand for Canadian dollars. If there are expectations that China will increase in growth, it will need more copper and therefore there will be a greater demand for Australian dollars, as Australia is a big exporter of copper. If there is a trade war between the USA and the rest of the world, though protectionist tariff policies are expected, some currencies will be weakened as their country's export potential is perceived to be weakened. Others may strengthen. For example, a tariff war between the USA and China will likely impact soybean prices and Brazil may benefit as a substitute exporter of soybeans to China, thus strengthening the Brazilian Real. In the longer term, the country that has stronger interest rates will have an edge in the competition for capital in-flows. This is also known as "the Carry Trade," which virtually disappeared after the 2008 financial collapse. But as global recovery occurs, this may very well be a major recurring phenomenon. From a general point of view, any projections or forecasts about economic growth in a country are actionable knowledge about the probable strengthening or weakening of a currency.

Global growth and estimates of global growth are taken into account by central banks. The reason is that central banks look to stimulate growth when needed, and to restrict growth when it threatens to exceed

Table 3.1 Japan low interest rates

Per annum percent	0.001

inflationary targets. Increasing the money supply and decreasing interest rates are the main tools used. This does not mean that they work directly. The transmission mechanism within an economy to affect central bank intentions is not direct and may often not work out as expected. The recent era of low interest rates and in fact negative rates (in Europe and Japan) have had a less than immediate stimulus effect (Table 3.1, Japan low interest rates). Even though the Federal Reserve, in response to the 08 collapse, significantly increased its balance sheet, by trillions of dollars, the real impact of printing money is less impactful until banks expand their loaning. It is estimated that of the total money supply, State money (money printed by the Feds) accounts for only 20% of the supply. Bank money (private money being lent out) accounts for 80%. The economist Steve Hanke, of Johns Hopkins University has underscored the critical role that Bank money has on stimulating economic activity or reducing it, when regulations restrict bank lending.

So, it is quite possible that the money supply does not reach as expected by a central bank, consumers, or corporations, through the credit market due to restrictions on lending and increased standards of risk control. This is known as a transmission problem and is an unsolved challenge of the central banks. In fact, the leading authority on measuring money supply, Professor Barnett, has argued that the Federal Reserve incorrectly measures the money supply (*Getting it Wrong: How Faulty Monetary Statistics Undermine the Fed, the Financial System and the Economy*).[1] The key point the forex trader needs to understand is that central bank policies are prone to error and even failure. It is important to watch whether the private money supply is actually reaching companies.

Sidebar: Measuring Money Supply

The Center for Financial Stability is the leading authority on measuring the money supply and is worth reviewing. (http://www.centerforfinancialstability.org/index.php)

---

[1] William A. Barnett, 2011. *Getting it Wrong.*

The End of the Era of QE

In any case, central bank stimulation known as quantitative easing (QE), with low to near zero interest rates dominated central banks from the 2008 Financial collapse to 2017 when interest rates started increasing again. The weakening of interest rates was so low, "that the yield on the worlds principal sovereign benchmark security made an 800 century low of 1.318% in July 2016" (Grant interest rate observer, December 1, 2017.) As of the beginning of 2018, the shift to increasing interest rates by the central banks is likely to continue. Which central bank will lead the way forward into 2018 and 2019 in this tightening? Which central banks will lag behind? The answers to these questions will help to shape prediction of the direction in currency pairs.

Inflation Targeting

Few traders who are alive today remember the time when inflation was soaring and a threat to the economy of the USA. We have to go back to the 1970s. But the era of increasing inflation may in fact be coming. Traders will need to update their knowledge base about economies and inflation. Basically, when economies are growing, the threat of an increasing rate of inflation becomes a front-burner issue for the markets. Central banks look to tighten monetary policy and increase interest rates to avoid overheating. *It is a balancing act.* Central banks have implemented a macro economic model where a 2% inflation target is accepted as the point at which an economy has a balance between growth, full employment without overheating into unacceptable inflation. That, at least, is the desire of the central banks.

When inflation data demonstrate low inflation pressures (keeping an economy below the 2% rate), central banks look to stimulate that economy by increasing the money supply (through asset purchases such as bonds), and by reducing interest rates. From a trader's perspective, if the market expects that the central bank will act to stimulate an economy, the currency will weaken because the expectation of stimulus goes in hand with an expectation of no increase in rates. In contrast, if the totality of data coming to the central bank indicates that an economy is growing, employment is strong, and wage growth is increasing, the central bank is generally going to seriously look at contracting policy mechanisms, reducing their bond purchases, and increasing interest rates. All of this is done to head off the overheating of that economy.

It is, however, often not a stimulus versus contraction choice. There is a third middle choice: *tapering*. Tapering is reducing stimulus by reducing the bond or asset purchases of the central bank. A central bank is not likely to go cold turkey from stimulus therapy. Instead, it chooses tapering. This is what the European Central Bank chose in the latter part of 2017 by reducing its bond purchases, but not yet increasing interest rates. In fact the ECB did announce in June of 2018 that they would end stimulus in December of 2018. But they did not forecast or project an increase in rates. The result has been greater volatility in the Euro currency.

Inflation Projections and Expectations are Key

Certainly inflation data and expectations about inflation are becoming more important and at the center of whether a currency will increase in value. Keep in mind that inflation forecasts are prone to error. It is not an exact science. In fact, the state of low inflation, even in the contexts of full employment in the USA, is an example of a disconnect between forecasts and what the models are predicting. Economic data is now more prone to error because of massive shifts in the global economy where technological innovation is suppressing prices.

It's important to note that deflation is often part of the scope of concern of the central banks. Deflation, which is the falling of prices, discourages consumers to save and avoid spending and therefore slows the economy even further. In particular, the Bank of Japan has been especially vigilant in fighting deflation. In response to deflation fears, the Bank of Japan has been aggressive in trying to stimulate the economy of Japan, to the extent of introducing negative interest rates. Here is what their monetary statement said on December 21, 2017:

At the Monetary Policy Meeting held today, the Policy Board of the Bank of Japan decided upon the following. (1) Yield curve control The Bank decided, by an 8-1 majority vote, to set the following guideline for market operations for the intermeeting period. [Note 1] The short-term policy interest rate: The Bank will apply a negative interest rate of minus 0.1 percent to the Policy-Rate Balances in current accounts held by financial institutions at the Bank. The long-term interest rate: The Bank will purchase Japanese government bonds (JGBs) so that 10-year JGB yields will remain at around zero percent. With regard to the amount of JGBs to be purchased, the Bank will conduct purchases at more or less the current pace – an annual pace of increase in the amount outstanding of its JGB holdings of about 80 trillion yen – aiming to achieve the target level of the long-term interest rate specified by the guideline. https://www.boj.or.jp/en/announcements/release_2017/k171221a.pdf

Brexit and Inflation

The reaction of the Sterling to the Brexit vote demonstrates a classic relationship between currency values and inflation. The shock wave of the Brexit vote caused an initial significant decline in the currency. After Brexit, the GBPUSD declined by nearly 11% causing an increase in inflation as imports became more expensive (Chart 3.1).

There are estimates that a decline of 10% in Sterling versus the euro increases UK prices by 3.8%.

A major reason that a trader should not ignore central bank statements is because the central bank does not want to surprise and disrupt markets. They need stability in markets and transparency in policy to enable the effective transmission of policy through the markets. A central bank shock is at all counts to be avoided. This makes central bank statements one of the most salient leading fundamental forces.

This does not mean that markets are not surprised when a central bank decision occurs. An excellent example is the Bank of England decision (November 2) to raise rates for the first time in ten years. Conventional wisdom would expect the currency to rise, since greater rates are attractive and should strengthen a currency. But in this case the Sterling fell. The reason was that the central bank gave the market no expectations of

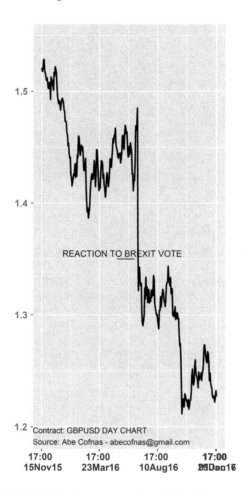

Chart 3.1   Initial GBPUSD shock wave reaction to Brexit

any near term further increase in rates. This is similar to when in the equity markets, a stock issues a strong earnings report, but the markets expect that it cannot continue to be that strong.

The point to keep in mind is that central bank statements, and often the news conferences that follow, unleash the important force of expectations. *Expectation uncertainty about what the central banks will do at their next scheduled rate deliberations causes the prices to move and change direction.* Once again, exclusive focus on technical analysis will fail to provide the trader the edge in trading central bank decisions.

4

How to Decode Central Bank Statements

We have noted that central bank statements are important to traders in shaping trading directional decisions. They can be called the Rosetta stone of forecasting currency price direction. But they need to be decoded. Let us explore how. The first approach is actually to read the central bank statements and minutes of their meetings. Over time one gets a sense of the core concerns of the central bank and whether they are in a stimulus, contraction, or holding pattern on interest rates. The trader can learn an enormous amount about fundamental forces by just reading and understanding the official statements and releases.

Let us look at the Bank of England statement of November 2, 2017, when they raised rates for the first time in ten years.[1]

The Bank of England's Monetary Policy Committee (MPC) sets monetary policy to meet the 2% inflation target, and in a way that helps to sustain growth and employment. At its meeting ending on 1 November 2017, the MPC voted by a majority of 7–2 to increase Bank Rate by 0.25 percentage points, to 0.5%. The Committee voted unanimously to maintain the stock of sterling non-financial investment-grade corporate bond purchases, financed by the issuance of central bank reserves, at £10 billion. The

---

[1] http://www.bankofengland.co.uk/publications/Pages/news/2017/007.aspx

© The Author(s) 2018
A. Cofnas, *Planet Forex*, https://doi.org/10.100//978-3-319-92913-2_4

Committee also voted unanimously to maintain the stock of UK government bond purchases, financed by the issuance of central bank reserves, at £435 billion.

We see immediately that the central bank has a focus on inflation and the inflation target is 2%!

In the MPC's central forecast, conditioned on the gently rising path of the bank rate implied by current market yields, GDP grows modestly over the next few years at a pace just above its reduced rate of potential. *Consumption growth remains sluggish* in the near term before rising, in line with household incomes. Net trade is bolstered by the strong global expansion and the past depreciation of Sterling. Business investment is being affected by the uncertainties around Brexit, but it continues to grow at a moderate pace, supported by strong global demand, high rates of profitability, the low cost of capital, and limited spare capacity.

The central bank is indicating no major shift in its forecasts.

CPI inflation rose to 3.0% in September. The MPC still expects inflation to peak above 3.0% in October, as the past depreciation of Sterling and recent increases in energy prices continue to pass through to consumer prices. The effects of rising import prices on inflation diminish over the next few years, and domestic inflationary pressures gradually pick up as spare capacity is absorbed and wage growth recovers. On balance, inflation is expected to fall back over the next year and, conditioned on the gently rising path of the bank rate implied by current market yields, to approach the 2% target by the end of the forecast period.

The central bank is giving no fear of an overheating economy.

The decision to leave the European Union is having a noticeable impact on the economic outlook. The overshoot of inflation throughout the forecast predominantly reflects the effects on import prices of the referendum-related fall in Sterling. Uncertainties associated with Brexit are weighing on domestic activity, which has slowed even as global growth has risen significantly. **And Brexit-related constraints on investment and labor supply appear to be reinforcing the marked slowdown that has been increasingly evident in recent years in the rate at which the economy can grow without generating inflationary pressures.**

The central bank is worried that Brexit might slow growth.

Unemployment has fallen to a 42-year low and the MPC judges that the level of remaining slack is limited. The global economy is growing strongly, domestic financial conditions are highly accommodative and consumer confidence has remained resilient. In line with the framework set out at the time of the referendum, **the MPC now judges it appropriate to tighten modestly the stance of monetary policy in order to return inflation sustainably to the target.**

The rate increase was justified as employment levels had reached historical highs.

We see in this classic statement from the Bank of England the mode of thinking that in fact all central banks employ regarding interest rate decisions. When economies are slowing down or weak, monetary and interest rate policies employ quantitative easing. When employment levels approach full employment and inflation reaches over 2%, quantitative tightening is the set of policy tools. It is a challenging balancing act.

> **Sidebar**
>
> Read https://www.inflationreport.co.uk/ to get a detailed perspective from the Bank of England.

Word Clouds

An additional valuable tool in filtering the central bank statement and gaining clarity can be the word cloud. Using word cloud generation software, (https://planetforex.shinyapps.io/wordcloud/) the following is a word cloud of the Bank of England Statement (Chart 4.1).

Chart 4.1   Bank of England statements and key word frequencies

Table 4.1 Bank of England statements and key word frequencies

Word	Count frequency (Sept 14 statement)	Count frequency (Nov 2 statement)
Inflation	13	13
Rate	9	7
Committee	9	None
Monetary	6	6
Policy	6	None
Target	6	None
Year	6	
Growth	5	None

The trader should practice word cloud generation as a tool for getting a sense of the changes in perspectives evidenced in the key statements of central banks.

Word Frequency Count

The next step in evaluating a central bank statement is the word frequency count. Using the same word cloud software, we can see that the word "inflate" is mentioned 13 times and is the most frequent word (Table 4.1). Clearly, for the Bank of England it is all about inflation. For the trader looking to trade the Sterling, it is all about knowing about inflation expectations.

Two Statement Comparison

The next step is to compare two statements by a central bank to detect any changes in emphasis and concern. Let us compare the statement of the Bank of England that raised rates for the first time in 10 years (November 2, 2017) and the statement of the preceding September Bank of England Statement (September 14, 2017).

Bank of England Word Cloud Comparison

A side-by-side word cloud comparison (Chart 4.2) easily shows that the key word change in the Bank of England's view of the economy between September 14, 2017, and November 2, 2017, was growth. The word

Chart 4.2   Bank of England statement word clouds

"Growth" is quite small in the September 14 statement. It was mentioned five times. Whereas it is obviously larger and was mentioned eight times on November 2. Words are powerful fundamental forces!

Central Bank Frequency Analysis

The following top ten words compare the September 14 and November 2 Bank of England statements shown in the word cloud above (Table 4.1).

Decoding Federal Reserve Statements

Always an important event in currency trading are the decisions of the Federal Reserve. The entire currency market focuses on the Federal Reserve Open Market Committee (FOMC) meetings and minutes "to read the tea-leaves" and try to shape expectations about whether the FOMC would implement its roadmap to increase rates. That path began at the end of 2016 and continued into 2018. Throughout this time, markets focused on whether interest rate increases would meet the projections that the Federal Reserve published. It is known as the dot plot. What the Federal Reserve does is important for more than just the USA. Every major central bank looks to what the Federal Reserve will do. After the Federal Reserve raised rates for the third time in December 2017, China's central bank raised rates. Why? To discourage capital outflow out of China into the USA.

For traders interested in getting into the details of how the Federal Reserve thinks about monetary policy, a great place to start is by reading the August 5, 2008 FOMC statement and then reading the statements of the FOMC after the collapse, leading on October 8 to a sudden dramatic 50 basis point drop in rates.

A good example of where the Federal Reserve revealed its "fears" occurs in the FOMC Minutes of the Federal Open Market Committee March 20–21, 2018. They note the uncertain impact of tariffs, and tax changes on the economic outlook. It is revealing that they chose to discuss these topics, *demonstrating that uncertainty is a major sentiment force.*

"A number of participants reported concern among their business contacts about the possible ramifications of the recent imposition of tariffs on imported steel and aluminum. Participants did not see the steel and aluminum tariffs, by themselves, as likely to have a significant effect on the national economic outlook, but a strong majority of participants viewed the prospect of retaliatory trade actions by other countries, as well as other issues and uncertainties associated with trade policies, as downside risks for the US economy. Contacts in the agricultural sector reported feeling particularly vulnerable to retaliation. Tax changes enacted in late 2017 and the recent federal budget agreement, taken together, were expected to provide a significant boost to output over the next few years. However, participants generally regarded the magnitude and timing of the economic effects of the fiscal policy changes as uncertain, partly because there have been few historical examples of expansionary fiscal policy being implemented when the economy was operating at a high level of resource utilization. A number of participants also suggested that uncertainty about whether all elements of the tax cuts would be made permanent, or about the implications of higher budget deficits for fiscal sustainability and real interest rates, represented sources of downside risk to the economic outlook. A few participants noted that the changes in tax policy could boost the level of potential output."

The take-away lesson from reading central bank statements is that learning what the central banks are worried about and what they are projecting improves the traders sense of currency direction. Careful reading of how the FOMC navigated through these times and the words that they used is invaluable in building a fundamental knowledge base for trading currencies (Table 4.2).

Finally, a great exercise for traders is to identify the fears of the central bank and then match those fears to probable policy actions (Table 4.3). We have noted that the greatest fear is inflation and the associated policy action is raising rates or monetary tightening. But raising rates implies an accurate projection on the future of inflation. If the central bank is wrong about that, it can lead to acting too late and overheating an economy causing a recession. It is a balancing act and not easy.

Beyond knowing how central banks think about the world, and knowing their fears, it is useful for the trader to further check a country comparison of key economic metrics. Such a comparative scan indicates which

Table 4.2 FOMC rate levels 2008 – June 13 2018

Jan 22, 08 3.50	22 Jan	2008	3.5
Jan 30, 08 3.00%	30 Jan	2008	3
Mar 18, 08 2.25	18 Mar	2008	2.25
Apr 30, 08 2.00	30 Apr	2008	2
Oct 8, 08 1.50	8 Oct	2008	1.5
Oct 29, 08 1.00	29 Oct	2008	1
Dec 16, 08 0.25	16 Dec	2008	0.25
Dec 16, 15 0.50	16 Dec	2008	0.5
Dec 14, 16 0.7	14 Dec	2008	0.75
Mar 15, 17 1.00	15 Mar	2008	1
Jun 14, 17 1.25	14 Jun	2008	1.25
Dec 13, 17 1.50	13 Dec	2008	1.5
Mar 21 1.75	21 Mar	2008	1.75

Table 4.3 Central quantitative easing deflation increased bank fears and likely decisions

Central bank fears	Likely action	Aggressive action
Inflation too low below 2%	Quantitative easing deflation increased	Reducing rates
Inflation exceeding 2%	Quantitative tightening	IIncreasing rates
Average hourly earnings up	No further easing	Quantitative easing
Average hourly earnings down	No further tightening	Quantitative easing
Full employment	Quantitative easing	Increasing rates
Flattening yield curve	No change in monetary policy	Quantitative easing
Inverted yield curve	Quantitative easing	Reducing rates
Tariff wars	Hesitation on policy changes	Hesitation on policy changes

Table 4.4 Key global economic metrics

	GDP	GDP YoY (%)	GDP QoQ (%)	Interest rate (%)	Inflation rate (%)	Jobless rate (%)
United States	18,624	2.6	2.90	1.75	2.40	4.10
Euro area	11,886	2.70	0.60	0.00	1.40	8.50
China	11,199	6.80	1.60	4.35	2.10	3.90
Japan	4940	2.00	0.40	−0.10	1.60	2.80
Germany	3467	2.90	0.60	0.00	1.80	3.60
United Kingdom	2648	1.40	0.40	0.50	4.30	4.30
Canada	1530	2.90	0.40	1.25	2.20	5.80
Australia	1205	2.40	0.40	1.50	1.90	5.60

Source: April 16, 2018 Tradingeconomics.com

currencies are likely to be getting stronger relative to other currencies. For example, look at Japan. At the end of 2017 it had an inflation rate of 0.20 and interest rates that were negative. The Yen, therefore, is likely to be very weak against other currencies. The Eurozone has an inflation rate at 1.4%, getting closer to the target 2%, but not quite there as the jobless rate is still very high at 8.5%. Therefore, the euro currency faces big headwinds against it strengthening. The UK, post-Brexit, suffered inflation that exceeded the target of 2%. Therefore, the Sterling is likely to face pressure against it strengthening. Of course, a currency pair has two sides and the cross pair is really a battle of expectations. The cross pair price code expectations of which country will grow relative to which will weaken, and which country's central bank is expected to increase, keep rates the same, or decrease them. A case in point is Australia, as US rates go up, the difference in the interest rates between the USA and Australia will narrow and therefore, weaken the Australian dollar as it loses its attractiveness as a carry trade. The Reserve Bank of Australia did not raise the rates during the whole of 2018 because of fears of a slowdown in consumer spending and the still high unemployment rate (Table 4.4).

Sidebar

Within a week of a central bank decision it is a good idea to check these economic metrics! A good source is: www.tradingmarkets.com

5

What is Sentiment?

The next step after gaining a knowledge base in fundamental analysis has to be converting that knowledge into action. A key weakness often mentioned in using fundamental analysis is that it is thought of as being too macro a viewpoint. Fundamental forces are perceived to not be actionable for day-to- day and minute-to-minute trading. This is a false viewpoint. Fundamental forces are not abstract concepts. They act on prices through a transmission mechanism: *sentiment.* Sentiment acts like gravity and exerts a force shaping price direction.

Applying the concept of sentiment provides a necessary increase in granularity to detect what is actually happening with price action. For example, the conventional description of a currency pair is that it is bullish or bearish. Traders describe prices as being in an uptrend, downtrend, or in consolidation. Further frequent descriptions are that the trend is being probed or broken. Moreover, the price may be in a bullish trend but retracing. All these descriptions are not inaccurate, but *they are* incomplete. These descriptions share a major weakness; they are low resolution and need a great deal more confirmation to become actionable in creating trading signals. A better approach is understanding sentiment as the energy behind the price action. The price action rides the sentiment.

© The Author(s) 2018
A. Cofnas, *Planet Forex*, https://doi.org/10.1007/978-3-319-92913-2_5

First, let us clarify what is meant by sentiment in this context. Sentiment is defined as containing a set of emotions. For example, a person can have a positive sentiment about an upcoming vacation. A trader can have a bullish sentiment about the direction of a price. Sentiments contain emotions which are about something. When we try to assess the sentiment that is being reflected in a currency pair, the trader needs to be careful in attributing the correct emotion to the price action. The currency pair, or market, does not have any emotion. Currency pairs have no goals. Currency pairs are not conscious entities. But they have a function, which is rather a reflection of emotions. Bullish or bearish patterns are caused by different sentiments or emotions result in the pushing and pulling of the price. It is a tug-of-war. Sideways patterns reflect a balance of expectations waiting for new catalysts to skew the sentiment. Currency pairs are seesaws of emotions reflecting an ongoing battle of expectations.

When sentiment analysis is used it brings an unprecedented depth of insight into price action. The language of sentiment analysis is itself different from the language and expressions emerging from candlestick analysis. With sentiment analysis one perceives markets. There are no bullish or bearish trends. Rather, there are bullish or bearish emotions and expectations. We can also call them bullish or bearish waves (or wavelets?). How these emotions are expressed will, of course, be detailed. This vantage point allows the trader to focus precisely on what the price is doing rather than where it may be going. Sentiment analysis filters out subjective factors and variables that would only distract the trader. With sentiment analysis the most important time frame is the now.

This focus on sentiment has a profound impact on trading tactics. The traders become like surfers; they spot a wave and jump on at the optimal point. They ride it without any predefined notion of how far they will ride that wave. This is hard to achieve psychologically. In fact, if the surfer had any a priori intentions on what that particular wave would be doing and how it would be moving, he would not last long. Another similar instructive example for forex traders is the western rodeo. Yes, watching a rodeo cowboy riding a bull and trying to last eight seconds without being thrown off is a remarkable example of sentiment-based tactics. The fact is that the cowboy is thrown off when he wrongly anticipates which way the animal will sway, and as a result is left on the floor. In a similar way, the forex sentiment trader can be understood as participating in a virtual forex rodeo, where putting on a trade is riding the bullish or bearish currency pair!

The forex trader who uses sentiment as the framework for trading is in every sense surfing forex sentiment waves or riding in an FX Rodeo! The exact trading tactics for sentiment trading are detailed in Chap. 6. For now, let us get a handle on visualizing sentiment.

Visualizing Sentiment

If currency pairs reflect sentiment, just how can the trader diagnose and detect the prevailing sentiment? Let us start with candlesticks; the commonly used representation of price action. Candlesticks (similarly, bar charts) show open, close, high and low, price points at any time slice (one minute, one hour, etc.) (Chart 5.1). Candlesticks, when grouped together, do provide a signature of a variety of emotions at that point in time. But they also generate a lot of noise. A famous candlestick, the Doji, provides a signature of hesitation. Yet it is not clear whether that emotion of hesitation is predictive of the coming moves.

The problem with candlesticks is that they generate a great deal of noise and a wide range of possible interpretations. Where is resistance? Is it above the high wicks or at the candle body close? Likewise, where is the support? Is it below the low wick, or is it at the low close? Subjective conclusions are clearly needed. An additional challenge of candlesticks is the difficulty in mastering all of the patterns and then converting that knowledge into tradeable action. Sentiment analysis presents an alternative to using candlesticks. The objective in using sentiment analysis is to filter the noise and to measure, more objectively, the degree of sentiment in the market. This alternative charting is known Line Break, and Renko charting. Let us explore some of the key features of these charts.

Line Chart
Line charts only show the close of the price and are like maps outlining boundaries in the price action (Chart 5.2).

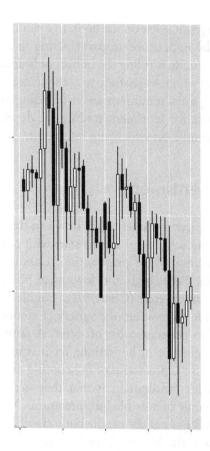

Chart 5.1 Candlesticks

Price Break Charting

Price break charting filters the price action in a specific way.

Here is how it works. The trader selects a slice of time, for example, one hour. Unlike candlesticks, the chart will only show whether the price has *closed* at a new high, or a new low. The chart system will check every hour. If there is a new low or a new high close, a line is added. This creates a block. If the price has not registered a new low or new high close, then no new line is added. So, we see in Chart 5.3 that the white blocks represent a new high close. All of the black blocks represent a new low close.

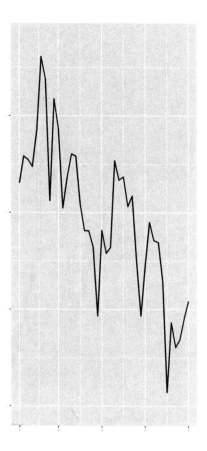

Chart 5.2 Line chart

Remember, it does not show how high or how low the price actually went (as the wicks in candlesticks do), it only shows the successful close. All we care about knowing is whether the price has had an ability to close higher or lower. Attempts by a price to go higher or lower, but only to close below the previous high or low close, are not recorded. Only *successful* attempts to achieve new high closes or new low closes are what these charts will show. We care about successful attempts at closing new high or new lows because this inherently represents a level of strength in the sentiment.

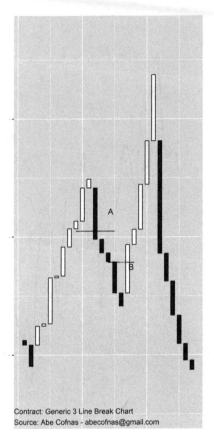

Contract: Generic 3 Line Break Chart
Source: Abe Cofnas - abecofnas@gmail.com

Chart 5.3   Generic price break chart

Reversal of Sentiment

Another key property of line break charts is the cause of a color change in
the block. A block will switch colors when a reversal of sentiment is trig-
gered. A bullish reversal of sentiment (black is followed by a white block;
Chart 5.3, Point B), occurs when the price closes above the three previous
high closes. A bearish reversal of sentiment (white is followed by a black
block; Chart 5.3, Point A), occurs when the price closes below the three
previous low closes. Line break charts are defaulted at three and therefore
the trader does not have to count the blocks.

A legitimate question is why is three lines the threshold used to trigger a reversal confirmation? The answer is that number three is common criteria for measuring a stable event. For example, three confirmations in technical analysis is considered sufficient to confirm a failure to break resistance or support. A triangle, with its three vertices, offers great stability. Three lines back provides a reasonable assurance that a reversal is strong enough and is in fact occurring. Setting the reversal threshold to four makes it a stronger confirmation because the price has to go further to trigger a reversal. However, it will require more time. Going down to two lines increases choppiness. Three lines is in the Goldilocks zone.

Why are line break charts so impactful?
By showing only whether the price is achieving a sequence of new high closes, or new low closes, the trader can instantly assess the strength of the sentiment. A strong bullish sequence will mean that the energy in the market has made it possible for the price to progressively and sequentially achieve new high closes. A strong bearish sequence, where there are several new low closes, instantly reveals that bearish emotions are in control. There is no ambiguity. *Candlesticks are not necessary.*

Line breaks provide a quick and objective view of bullish and bearish and reversal conditions, for any time frame, from a day to one minute, sentiment can be measured.

Let us explore the following example of a multi-time frame sequence of line break visuals for the currency pair USDJPY. We will evaluate and compare the day, four-hour, one-hour, 15-minute, five-minute, and one-minute line break charts.

Day 3 Line Break Chart

Starting with the day time frame (Chart 5.4), we see that the three-line breaks clearly show a sequence of bearish new low day closes, followed by a larger reversal (white block). The bullish sentiment is therefore strong. The trader looking for a direction has permission to look for a buy. Remember that each block is NOT registering one day. It only registers when a new day high or low close has occurred or reversed.

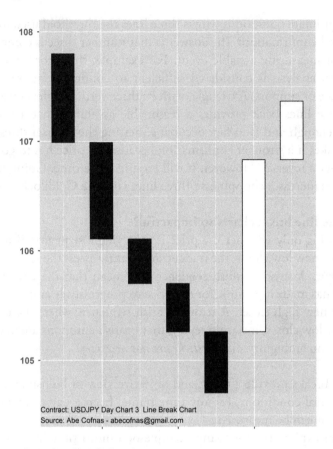

Contract: USDJPY Day Chart 3 Line Break Chart
Source: Abe Cofnas - abecofnas@gmail.com

Chart 5.4 Three-line break day chart

Four-Hour 3 Line Break Chart

The next step is to scroll down a time frame to a slightly lower slice of time than one day. Some traders can choose eight hours, six hours, or even four hours. The point is to get some further confirmation of the sentiment that is dominating the market. Did the sentiment shift? Let us look at the four-hour, three-line (Chart 5.5).

This time frame visualizes whether the price is able to be persistently closing new four-hour highs, or new four-hour lows. This four-hour

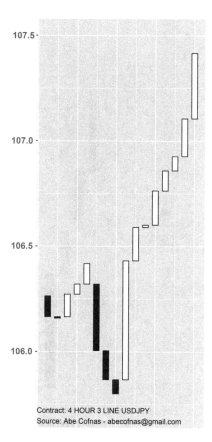

107.5
107.0
106.5
106.0

Contract: 4 HOUR 3 LINE USDJPY
Source: Abe Cofnas - abecofnas@gmail.com

Chart 5.5   Three-line break four-hour chart

three-line shows a strong sequence of new high closes. In fact, there were eight sequential new four-hour high closes, which is very powerful! The trader can conclude that the sentiment is sustaining a bullish move. There is no strong evidence of any bearish sentiment at this point. A willingness to buy is supported.

JUST when would a trader look to be buying? Not yet. We need to drill down to a shorter time frame that allows us to diagnose the more near term sentiments that are acting upon the prices. Let us drill down further to a one-hour, three-line (Chart 5.6).

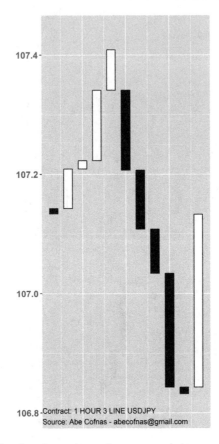

107.4

107.2

107.0

106.8 Contract: 1 HOUR 3 LINE USDJPY
Source: Abe Cofnas - abecofnas@gmail.com

Chart 5.6   Three-line break one-hour chart

The one-hour chart shows an interesting dynamic. We see that there was a bearish push down with five consecutive one-hour new low closes. But the bullish sentiment was countered and was strong enough to cause a reversal back towards the direction of the four-hour bullish sentiment. *This is very significant.* A one-hour reversal into the direction of the four-hour line break chart can be an immediate buy order! We have an alignment of a lower time frame with the direction of the higher time frame! Such an alignment is a key principle of trading with sentiment analysis. Does the trader stop at the 1 hour 3 line break chart, or should there be further magnification of the sentiment at lower time slices such as the 5 minute or 1 minute 3 line break charts? The answer depends on whether one is trading intra-week, intra-day, or even intra-hour. As the trading duration reduces, the time frame appropriate to use can be lower than 1 hour. But the key principle is an alignment of a lower 3 line break time frame with a higher 3 line break time frame.

Line break charts are powerful detectors of sentiment conditions and effectively guide traders to being on the right side of the direction.

Renko Bricks

A visualization of sentiment is not complete without detecting whether the price can move in persistent distances. While a line break shows only movements of new high, new low closes, and reversals, Renkobricks show the capabilities of the price to move a predetermined measured distance. The question that Renko bricks answer is whether the price is able to move in a sequence of five, or ten bricks. The time setting recommended is one minute to achieve a high resolution of whether the direction is changing. If the feed is a tick feed, then the setting can be at a tick level. The reason for a 10-pip setting as a default is to obtain evidence at a micro level of what the sentiment is and whether there is a gathering threat.

For gold, oil, and other indexes, the settings should be a percentage of the price, such as 1%.

In the example of Chart 5.7 one can immediately see, without the noise of candles, that the price action is persisting in a bullish direction. It's important to note that this is a snapshot, and in real time a Renko brick will not form until there is movement in either direction of the prescribed distance (10 pips).

There are several benefits of looking at Renko charts. First, they filter out the noise within a time frame that is considered quite noisy using candlesticks. For example, look at the comparison of the one minute candlesticks with the one minute Renko bricks at a 10-pip size setting (Chart 5.7). The candlestick chart shows swings and gives the impression of uncertainty in the bullish move up. Whereas, in contrast, the Renko charts show no interruption of the bullish persistence. They filter out the noise. A more accurate depiction of sentiment strength of the

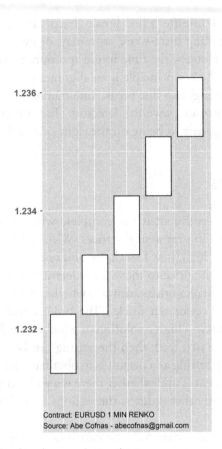

Contract: EURUSD 1 MIN RENKO
Source: Abe Cofnas - abecofnas@gmail.com

Chart 5.7 Three-line break one-minute chart

price movement is being shown and quantified. *Sentiment becomes understood as the ability of a currency pair to move a predetermined size, per minute!*

Comparison of Candles and Renko

Let us explore, from a biological perspective, why sentiment analysis using Renko bricks is effective. If one went to the doctor and had an infection, a lab test by measuring the white cell count would show if the infection was declining or increasing. Similarly, Renko bricks provide a visualization of the sentiment against an existing trade. It is a virtual lab test of the threat to the health of the trade! Consider the situation where a trader is long a currency pair and has reached a level of profits in pips that causes the trader to want to take the profits. Most traders would exit a position once it has reached a predetermined take profit target, only to see that the position continued to higher levels of profits. With Renko bricks the trader can easily determine if the micro-sentiment was, in fact, in the trader's direction. The trader would stay in until the bricks showed movement the other way!

The Fundamental Knowledge Grid

By combining fundamental with sentiment analysis, we can now complete the Fundamental Knowledge Grid (Table 5.1). This is inspired by the work of Abraham Maslow. He is famous for his hierarchy of needs describing the priorities that humans face, from needing food to actualizing their personalities. Likewise, our claim is that there is a hierarchy of knowledge currency traders need to actualize on their path to professional trading. We can call it the Fundamental Knowledge Grid. It describes the core components of fundamental analysis and tops it off with understanding sentiment conditions and sentiment alignments, leading to the trading signal. Navigating this hierarchy of knowledge about fundamentals and sentiment the trader will be ready for trading the currency markets.

Table 5.1 Fundamental Knowledge Grid

Hierarchy of sentiment analysis	Key questions
Trading signal confidence	What is your ranking of the alignment from a scale of 1–5
Sentiment alignment	Is the lower line break chart aligned with the higher line break chart and with the Renko bricks?
Sentiment conditions	Are equity markets risk-on, or risk-off?
Balance of fears	Is there a fear of inflation, stagflation, deflation, recession? Or geopolitical risks?
Central bank policies	Is the central bank in an easing, neutral, or tightening mode?

6

Sentiment Trading Set-Ups

What is a signal?

The act of putting on a trade implies that there is a trading signal that has been detected. Just what is a signal? The best approach to understanding a signal is that it is a change in conditions, a break of a pattern. This is common sense and part of our daily experience. When driving a car on the highway, we do not notice all of the details of all of the cars near us. We only pay attention when a car in front of us is swerving. It is a break in the pattern. It is a signal to act upon. From a sentiment point of view, a signal is a change in the sentiment direction and in the particular alignment of sentiment in multiple time frames. Signals and set-ups can be sorted into two types: Position Trading Signals and Momentum Trading Signals.

Position Trading Sentiment Set-Ups

A position trade is characterized by a longer duration where the trader is riding a strong sentiment force. Positions can have durations of going beyond a day and sometimes can be several weeks. Sentiment analysis can assist the trader in pinpointing the direction and where to enter.

At least two time frames are necessary for a sentiment position trade. First a higher time frame and then a lower time frame. The higher time

© The Author(s) 2018
A. Cofnas, *Planet Forex*, https://doi.org/10.1007/978-3-319-92913-2_6

frame provides a background verification of the strength and direction of the sentiment. A lower time frame provides a trigger for entry. Three duration views are also acceptable and provide extra granularity for detecting sentiment. The key point is to enter only in the direction of the higher time frame. Deciding which time frames should be used depends a great deal on the style of the trading. A position trader, looking for inter-week positions might choose a weekly duration as the higher time frame, and a daily duration as a lower time frame. A day and a two hour is another combination. A six hour and a 30 minute combination is also worth exploring.

How about timing the entry? If a trader wants to go long, should the chart be pointing into an upward direction? If a trader wants to go short, should the chart be pointing into a downward direction? The answer is not that straightforward. The critical factor for entry is the condition that prices, even though are moving in a certain direction, have had a pull-back which is followed by a reversal back in the prior direction. In other words, the price tried to reverse direction, it did, but failed and swung back. *The swing back makes the optimal entry point the moment when the prices are moving back toward the higher time frame direction!* This can be called a U-turn, named after a car shifting directions from going one way to the opposite way. Hopefully, it is a legal U-turn.

A good way to visualize the power of the U-turn as a trading signal is the analogy of a car moving fast approaching a curve. The angular momentum makes it difficult for the car to slow down and straighten out. Similarly, when a price pulls back and then turns back around, the energy is of high momentum and is likely to carry the price much further. A U-turn or swing back shown in 3 line break charts provide a high-level of confirmation that sentiment has reversed and into the higher 3 line break time frame.

Sentiment Alignments for Position Trading

Let us examine several snapshots of possible alignments for a sentiment position trade, and explore which alignments offer a high probable position trade set-up.

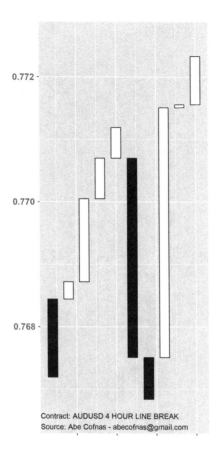

Chart 6.1 AUDUSD four-hour line break

Sentiment condition: Conflict between one-hour and four-hour sentiment: No condition to trade.

In the following chart (Chart 6.1) we can see that the four-hour, three-line break chart for the AUDUSD is showing a sequence of three consecutive new four-hour high closes. This is depicted in white. We see a large white line break reversal followed by a thin new four-hour high close. But then it was followed by a bigger move to a new high close. Seeing this condition, the trader is biased to be looking for a buying opportunity.

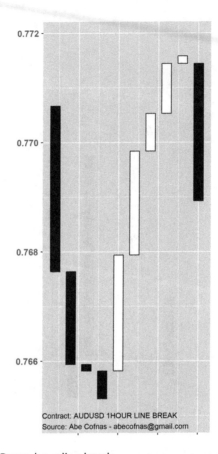

Chart 6.2   AUDUSD one-hour line break

A next step would be to monitor what the one-hour three-line conditions are (Chart 6.2). The most important condition to detect is whether the lower time frame, in this case the one hour, is aligned in the same direction of the higher time frame (four hour). The latest line break pattern on the one hour AUDUSD is clearly black and therefore it is *not aligned*. Going long is not permitted. The trader would have to wait for the one hour to reverse back into the direction of the four hour, three line.

Sentiment condition: Alignment between four-hour and one-hour three-line break: With alignment of a lower one-hour line break.

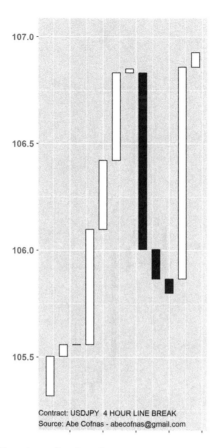

107.0

106.5

106.0

105.5

Contract: USDJPY 4 HOUR LINE BREAK
Source: Abe Cofnas - abecofnas@gmail.com

Chart 6.3   USDJPY four-hour line break

In this next example of an alignment match we see clearly that the four-hour USDJPY (Chart 6.3) is bullish having had a strong white line break reversal followed by a second new high close. This followed a sequence of bearish black line breaks. The trader can immediately conclude that there is permission to buy and the bullish sentiment is strong. But the next step is to see if there is an alignment of the lower one-hour line break (Chart 6.4) in the same direction of the four-hour line break chart. The trader seeing this alignment can enter the trade at the market because the bullish sentiment has reversed in the direction of the higher time frame, and in fact is pushing higher.

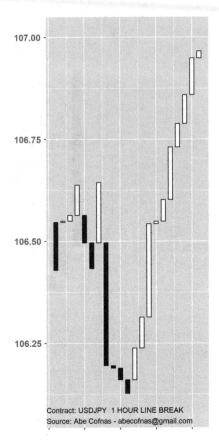

Chart 6.4 USDJPY one-hour line break bullish alignment with higher signal

Sentiment condition: Bearish alignment.

Let us consider a scenario where there is a bearish alignment between a lower and higher time frame (Chart 6.5).

The four-hour three-line pattern shows a reversal of sentiment into a bearish direction with three consecutive new low four-hour closes. The task now is to go to the lower time frame and see if it is aligned.

In this case, we can see that the lower five-minute three-line GBPNZD pattern had a sequence of bullish moves, and then a bearish reversal (Chart 6.6). It therefore aligns with the higher four-hour time frame. It is a signal to go short at the market. It is a strong signal because the lower time frame

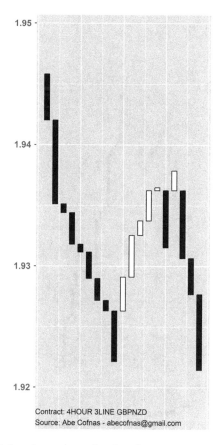

Chart 6.5 GBPNZD four-hour three-line break

has experienced a reversal 3 line break in the direction of the higher time frame. This is an optimal moment to catch. It is useful to note, that even if the trader misses the close of the lower time frame reversal, if the next 3 line close follows in the direction, it is an acceptable trading entry.

What about Limits and Stops

In a position sentiment trade, when the excursion of the trade takes time, it incurs the increased risk of being wrong. A position trade is difficult to watch as traders are busy and also reluctant to be slaves to the screen. Therefore, the trader needs to not only ride the direction of sentiment, but also needs to ride the mathematics of the profitability curve. An

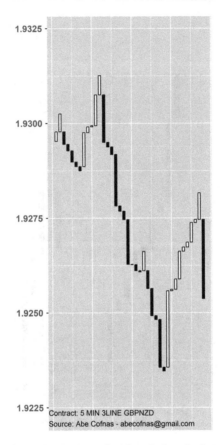

Chart 6.6   GBPNZD five-minute three-line break signals short

initial good place to determine a stop and limit strategy is to commit to a reward to risk ratio of 2:1 The trader would put on the market order, for example, to sell, and locate a stop above the previous high close (the white candle before the reversal). The distance between the stop and the market order is the risk and it can vary. The key point is that once the stop is selected, the risk is calculated. Let us call it X. The take profit target in the position trade should at least be 2X.

This ratio should be the standard applied to each trade. Why? It is because if one is 50% right in the trade, the approach is profitable. Most traders have little patience to do a "stress-test" on their trading strategies. It is a good idea to take the measure of one's performance, every ten trades, and quantify the average profit per trade, and the average risk per trade. Does it match the 2:1 target? Each ten trade series provides a check-up on the health of the strategy. The downside of this approach is the human factor, where traders have no patience and are not disciplined to stick to the rules. Actually, an effective quick improvement in performance will be accomplished by moving the original stop loss to a break-even position. Then the trader has a free ride!

By using the mathematics of profitability as a key rule for placing limits and stops, the trader still needs to locate the initial stop and limit, if a position trade is being used. A good approach is to put on a market order to buy when a new high close occurs *on the lower time frame*. The stop would be then below the previous low close. How far below? Enough to allow the market to vibrate. Then the limit would be located 2× the risk distance. Selling is just the exact opposite. The sell order is placed at the close that the three-line has turned from a bull into the bearish direction (black). The stop is located above the previous high close, and the sell limit target is simply 2× the risk (Chart 6.7).

This is simple mathematics. What we are saying is that the goal is to achieve profitability with 50% being right as a first step. After that, optimizing the performance can occur in many ways by examining alternative time frames, and market situations. But profitability is the first goal of any trading.

Back Tests

It is useful to get a sense of the profitability potential of using line break position trading described in this chapter. In this example (Table 6.1), the strategy was back tested using the four-hour three-line, and one-hour three-line, on the GBPJPY as a trigger. This was a set-and-let strategy. We let the system work on its own. No stops were moved to a break-even point.

In Table 6.1 we did a back test on the GBPJPY using the four-hour three-line, and one-hour three-line strategy. It met the important parameters of profitability. The average win/loss ratio was 16:15, which is essentially break even. However, the average winning pips was 92 versus the average losing pips of −50. The wins were 1.84 × the average loss, generating a profitable system. Once again, keep in mind that this is an

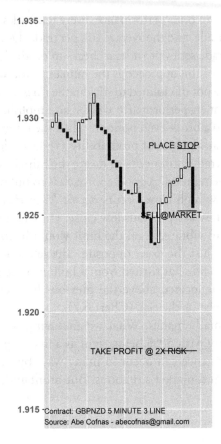

Chart 6.7 Stops and limits

Table 6.1 Back test GBPJPY August 7–November 14, 2017

Total trades	31
Net pips	729
Total winning trades	16
Net winning pips	1483
Average winning pips	92
Total losing trades	15
Net losing pips	−754
Average losing pips	−50
Net %P/L	5.0819

Source: www.smarttick.com

Table **6.2** Back test GBPUSD four-hour three-line, and one-hour three-line, August 3, 2017–November 17, 2017

Total trades	35
Net pips	425
Total winning trades	14
Net winning pips	1214
Average winning pips	86
Total losing trades	21
Net losing pips	−789
Average losing pips	−37
Average gain/average loss	2.324324

Source: www.smartick.com

unmanaged result. No stops were moved to break even, which would significantly increase the overall profitability.

Another back test was of the GBPUSD using a four-hour three-line, and a one-hour three-line for alignment. In this case we had a win/loss ratio that is actually negative (14 wins/21 losing trades). But the average gain/average loss was quite large: 86/37 for a ratio of 2.3. It is useful to note that this was totally unmanaged (Table 6.2).

These back tests suggest that the potential of profits aligning a lower with a higher three-line break time frame is strong. The most important testing is forward testing of these strategies. The best way to do this is in a live account trading at only 1:1 leverage. For example, a 10,000 account would permit a nominal position size of 10,000 on a trade. This is commonly known as a mini-lot. A standard lot is 100,000 generating a value of approximately $10 per pip. This may vary slightly depending on the currency pair traded.

Momentum Sentiment Trading: FX Rodeo

Momentum sentiment trading is one of the most exciting set-ups and is the opposite of position trades. It requires *no target, no limits*, and *no stops!* It is purely riding the sentiment wave! In it, the trader *experiences* the sentiment rather than analyzes it. Another way to understand the basics of this momentum set-up is through the analogy of the rodeo. In the classic American cowboy western rodeo, the cowboy sits on a bull locked in behind a gate. The gate opens and the cowboy is challenged to stay on that bull until it throws him off! In these bull-riding rodeos, eight seconds is considered to be champion duration. What is most interesting is that the cowboy gets thrown off when he anticipates the underlying movement of the bull. If the bull surprises the cowboy and sways another way, he is thrown off. So, let us visualize a sentiment trade as an FX Rodeo. The underlying currency pair is the animal. If we are buying the USDJPY, then one can call it a dollar bull ride. If one is selling the USDJPY, then one can call it a yen bull ride. That keeps the analogy intact!

Before we trigger the entry, first we need to confirm that there is an alignment of sentiment of the lower time frame with the higher time frame. But the critical momentum trade signal is when the one-minute Renko aligns with the five-minute three-line. For this sentiment wave rider, or FX Rodeo strategy, a five-minute three-line chart would be very useful. We can see that the five-minute three-line is USDCAD.

We want to ensure that at a micro-detection level, there is also the same sentiment to enter the position. To do this we turn to the Renko bricks.

Let us look at a trade trigger using Renko. The trader in Chart 6.8 is looking to sell and the trigger condition would be only if the Renko bricks had shifted from a sequence of white bricks to black bearish bricks. The trader seeing this shift can enter a sell trade in the market. The alignments are solid as the one-minute Renko is confirming a persistence down and is aligned with the five-minute three-line. The five-minute three-line is assumed to be aligned with a higher time frame. A buy trigger is exactly the opposite with the 10 pip Renko bricks shifting into a bullish reversal with one or two bricks breaking out of resistance (Chart 6.8). It is useful to note that there is not a prescribed number of Renko bricks that would trigger an entry or an exit. The key is whether the price has shown a confirming shift in direction.

Where are the Stops and Limits?
One might be tempted to ask: where are the stops, where are the targets? How does one stay on the trade? The trader simply stays on until there is evidence against the direction. The evidence is the emergence of Renko bricks in the opposite direction of the trade. As soon as a Renko brick 10 pips is closed of the opposite color, jump off. This means, realistically, that the risks to the trade is 10–15 pips because of possible slippage movement. It also means that the sentiment direction can continue to go a significant distance into very nice profits of 50 or more pips!

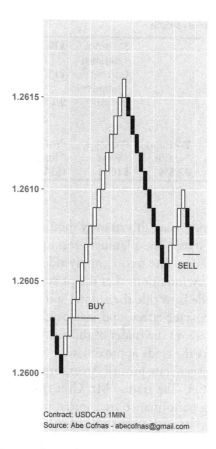

Contract: USDCAD 1MIN
Source: Abe Cofnas - abecofnas@gmail.com

Chart 6.8 USDCAD one-minute three-line break

An important effect of this strategy is also how it augments profits. Consider the dilemma facing the forex trader when the trade reaches a target level. Should he get out? Most traders just get out when they reached a target. This has a logic to it, but it is flawed because the reason to get out should be when there is evidence of a rising threat against the position. Since commonly used technical analysis set-ups simply provide a target, it is understandable that a trader gets out when the target is reached. But it is not optimal. Too often getting out at a take profit limit leaves money on the table as the price continues to go in the direction of more profits. With the one-minute 10 pip Renko bricks the trader can stay in longer beyond a target.

Table 6.3 Performance example

Total trades	40			Starting balance	$10,250		
Average position	24,775			Current balance	$11,185		
Total profit	$935			% return	9.1%		
Avg profit per trade	$23.37						
Winning trades	Losing trades	Winning trade %	Profits – wins	Profits – losses	Average $/win	Average $/loss	
33	7	82.5%	$1080	($145)	$33	($21)	

Source: Abe Cofnas

The take-away from using this strategy should be that it is a pure price action/momentum trade. The alignment sets up the trade, but the entry is pure Renko breakout. The trader simply rides the sentiment, without being encumbered by intentions. Let the price action work its way. The only task of the trade is to ride the animal spirit of the market! There is one more very important effect, and it is psychological. The sentiment momentum trade relieves the trader of the burden of too much thinking and analytics. In fact the trade approximates pure experience.

Does this strategy generate profits? An example of a real trading record is shown in Table 6.3. The trader, Mr. G, a student of this technique, shows the following performance after initial training. From a period of April 2 to April 11, 40 trades were placed using the rules of FX Rodeo Momentum trading described in this chapter. We have an excellent performance of 82.5% winning trades, and an average gain/average loss ratio of 1.4. The challenge ahead for this trader is to maintain this record as he takes on bigger positions.

7

Cryptocurrencies

We cannot conclude our analysis of fundamental forces and sentiment trading without a reference to cryptocurrencies (Bitcoin, Ethereum, Litecoin, and so on).

> Bubbles are not just about the madness of crowds—nor are they simply mani-festations of excess liquidity and leverage. But both of these factors are present in the extraordinary rise of bitcoin over recent months. Every spectacular bub-ble involves a premonition of the future. The trouble is that they turn out to be deeply flawed premonitions. In this respect, bitcoin has much in common with great historic speculative manias. Edward Chancellor (https://www.reuters. com/article/us-markets-bitcoin-breakingviews/breakingviews-chancellor-bit-coin-speculators-face-total-wipeout-idUSKBN1E721S, December 13, 2017)

What are cryptocurrencies? The answer is not that straightforward. Are they commodities? Are they money? The best way to understand them is that they are digitized assets, with blockchain algorithms that eliminate the need for a central counterparty to make an exchange. From a regulatory point of view, different countries have different ways of defining them.

See https://www.loc.gov/law/help/bitcoin-survey. Platforms are also emerging that allow trading of cryptocurrencies. (www.binance.com)

© The Author(s) 2018
A. Cofnas, *Planet Forex*, https://doi.org/10.1007/978-3-319-92913-2_7

Going beyond the esoteric and regulatory arguments about the nature of cryptocurrencies, the focus here is on how to trade them. The best approach is using sentiment analysis. The best way to understand them, is that they are a manifestation of crowd behavior. It makes a lot of sense, as buyers of cryptos are buying because others are buying, and sellers are selling because others are selling. We are witnessing a virtual swarm movement.

The challenge to the trader is *when to fade or follow the crowd*. This is not an easy challenge as crowd mania makes traditional technical analysis unable to reliably analyze the patterns. But sentiment analytics using price break charts acts as a filter and can provide insight into when to enter or exit crypto currencies. It is precisely because the crypto underlying markets are sentiment based, that our price break visualizations can be an effective guide on how to trade them, for those who want to take on more than the usual risk. Let us explore this in detail.

Steps in Trading Crypto

Assuming that one has already obtained access to cryptocurrencies through a wallet, the first challenge is that of selection. Just which of the hundreds of Cryptocurrencies should one trade? There were, on April 11, 2018, 1566 cryptocurrencies listed at www.coinmarketcap.com. How can a trader make sense of this large domain and select trading opportunities?

Selecting the Crypto to Trade

There are uncountable approaches to trading cryptos. Some traders see them as similar to penny stocks and look for a very small priced crypto, such as below $1 and look to catch a large jump. It is important to keep in mind that the price at these low levels may actually reflect a lack of value, or perhaps ignorance about the potential. Another approach is to select those cryptos that have achieved a reasonable level of capitalization such hundreds of millions of dollars. Capitalization offers at least a modicum of rationality as it demonstrates that there is a crowd forming around that crypto. But once a crypto is selected a key filter is diagnosing the pattern. Is it demonstrating a buy or a sell opportunity?

Let us look at the top ten crypto currencies and compare their patterns using three-line break analysis.

Bitcoin

Bitcoin is the most commonly known cryptocurrency. Its market cap reached $117,633,712,941 with 16,971,525 coins produced. However, it has a maximum supply of 21,000,000.

While hindsight is 20/20 vision, insight is not. Insight into bitcoin (as well as other cryptos) can be used to identify in advance locations for entry that are optimal and exits that are advisable from a risk point of view. This can be achieved by converting the price action into sentiment visuals. Let us go through the process.

In Chart 7.1 we see the historical rise and fall of bitcoin. It shows a bitcoin day pattern and when viewed in terms of volatility, we see it has had ranges of 30% in a day! It is not for the timid (Chart 7.2).

Candlestick and Bitcoin

Let's zoom in on bitcoin from a three-line break perspective (Chart 7.3).

The immediate ability to see that there is a persistence of sentiment is of great interest. Bearish new low day closes of three or more days in a row of new low day closes can be seen. Also of great interest are the reversal patterns. When bitcoin reversed back into being bullish, there is no long sequence of white bullish new high closes. The reversals are swing failures. Using this analysis, we can formulate a strategy for trading bitcoin:

1. detect major sentiment direction;
2. enter the market only after a reversal color has appeared and has been followed by another reversal back into the main direction. We can see in Chart 7.4 some of these key reversal areas.

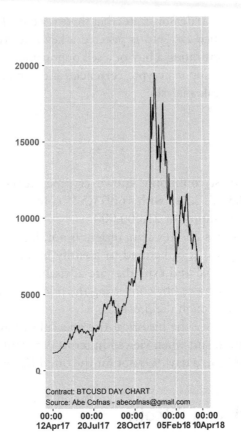

Chart 7.1 Bitcoin day chart

Finally, let us evaluate the price patterns from a line break perspective.

We can see clearly whether the sentiment is bullish or bearish and, importantly whether it is persisting. We can see where it is strong enough to reverse and change color.

This strategy rides the sentiment wave when it is optimal; when the price pulls back and then recovers to take out the previous three-line high close! So we only enter on these conditions. We take profit when we achieve 2× and 3× the risk. This allows for large profits, and gets us out of the way. From a trading mind-set, this rule tells the trader to jump on a crypto only when it has demonstrated the ability to recover from a reversal being expressed as a 3 line break chart. This can be a Day 3 line break or lower time frames! Always trade with the prevailing direction.

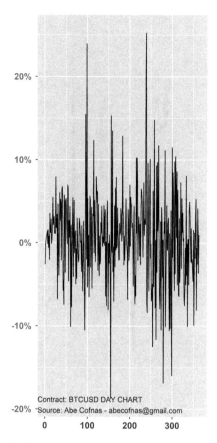

Chart 7.2 Bitcoin volatility

Ethereum

Ethereum is a contending cryptocurrency that can also be traded. As of April 2018 it had a market cap of $41,394,737,549.

Let us look at the price pattern from a three-line break perspective. See https://www.ethereum.org/

The three-line break chart of Ethereum four-hour pattern shows that the sentiment is generally bullish (Chart 7.5).

Bearish swings have failed to be sustained. A strategy for trading Ethereum based on the pattern exhibited is to buy it right after the

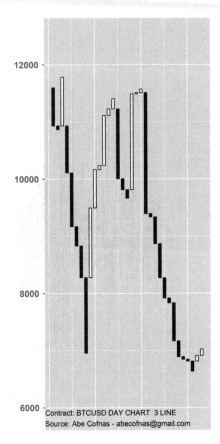

Contract: BTCUSD DAY CHART 3 LINE
Source: Abe Cofnas - abecofnas@gmail.com

Chart 7.3 Bitcoin day three-line break

three-line reverses back into a bullish new high close. The trader would apply our concept of a lower time frame aligned with a higher time frame. Looking at the one-hour, three-line pattern, we can see that it is exhibiting a sequence of new high closes (Chart 7.6).

The one-hour, three-line entry point would be after a swing failure down, and the black line appears, which is followed by a reversal white line. The trader could go and buy at the market at the close of the one-hour three-line break (Chart 7.7).

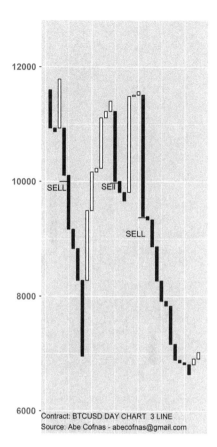

Contract: BTCUSD DAY CHART 3 LINE
Source: Abe Cofnas - abecofnas@gmail.com

Chart 7.4   Bitcoin key reversal areas shown with three-line break

Ripple

Ripple is a popular cryptocurrency with a very low price, but still with a high market cap of $19,872,917,668. This makes it very interesting. The price pattern shows that it, like bitcoin, has large swings.

The three-line break chart hour (Chart 7.8) shows a sideways pattern that encountered a bullish breakout. The signal to buy was on the close of the bullish line. With a crypto in a low price range of Ripple, many

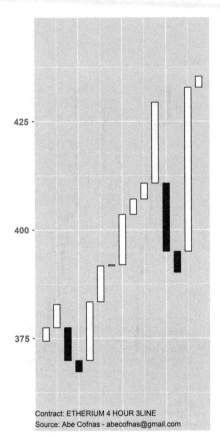

Contract: ETHERIUM 4 HOUR 3LINE
Source: Abe Cofnas - abecofnas@gmail.com

Chart 7.5 Ethereum four-hour three-line break

traders are looking to buy and hold, and three-line provides a good way
of locating where to put on a position.

What is the "Smart Money" Doing?

Beyond selecting cryptos based on their sentiment patterns, it is important to focus on those that have attracted "smart" money. Using a leaderboard of cryptos we can select those that are in the top tiers of capitalization.
For example, we can see in the table below the top 20 cryptos by how
much capital they attracted. Bitcoin remains (as of January 8, 2018), the

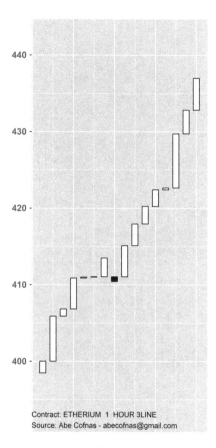

Contract: ETHERIUM 1 HOUR 3LINE
Source: Abe Cofnas - abecofnas@gmail.com

Chart 7.6   Ethereum one-hour three-line

leader in capitalization with $255 billion. But look at Ripple, which has $98 0.6 billion! Also notice that Ripple is priced at an affordable, low price of $98. A billion other cryptos in the top 20 are also at extremely low prices. This provides another filter: Price. The trader can put together an affordable low set of lower priced, highly capitalized cryptos with large potential. In short, there are three filters for choosing to trade cryptos:

1. Check the leaderboard on capitalization
2. Choose a diversified set of cryptos with lower prices.
3. Evaluate their three-line break patterns to decide whether there are buying or selling opportunities.

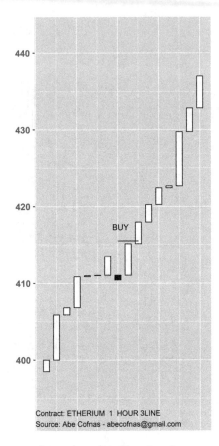

Chart 7.7 Ethereum one-hour three-line buy signal

Name	Market cap	Price
Bitcoin	$255,856,347,501	$15,238.40
Ethereum	$112,066,521,861	$1157.06
Ripple	$98,608,168,859	$2.55
Bitcoin Cash	$40,939,155,739	$2422.36
Cardano	$23,913,081,626	$0.92
NEM	$14,944,499,998	$1.66
Litecoin	$14,087,705,647	$257.68
Stellar	$11,721,028,540	$0.66
IOTA	$10,858,151,665	$3.91
TRON	$10,118,581,074	$0.15
Dash	$8,679,640,862	$1111.89
NEO	$6,816,160,000	$104.86

(continued)

(continued)

Name	Market cap	Price
Monero	$6,143,884,540	$394.39
EOS	$5,720,132,533	$9.68
Qtum	$4,223,687,599	$57.24
Bitcoin Gold	$4,051,559,161	$241.84
ICON	$4,002,015,647	$10.57
Lisk	$3,716,118,813	$31.82
RaiBlocks	$3,584,965,273	$26.90
Ethereum Classic	$3,466,670,834	$35.03

Trading cryptos is likely to be part of the new digital trading landscape. *Yet, we conclude from a fundamental point of view, that they reflect crowd behavior, and as a result using sentiment methodologies will provide an edge to trading them*

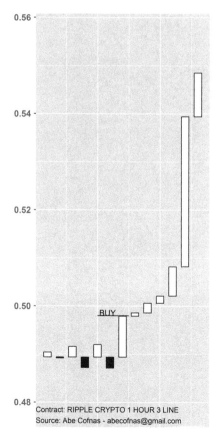

Chart 7.8 Ripple one-hour three-line

8

The Future of Forex Trading: Algorithms, Artificial Intelligence, and Social Forex Trading

In the 24/7 increasingly fast-paced world of geopolitical events, trading currencies requires the monitoring and absorption of a great deal of data. In previous decades, the knowledge necessary to evaluate market conditions depended on fewer variables and forex trading was less influenced by global events. The globalization of communications through the internet enables instant transmission of data, noise, and emotions. It is more difficult than ever to separate the signal from the noise. Where once price filters were enough, today, event filters and emotional filters are necessary. The markets are open systems and are almost irreducibly complex. The human currency trader is more limited than ever in absorbing global data. Certainly, the use of systems to assist human trading is the future of trading. In fact, many references point to the fact that 70% of all trading is algorithmic. Further confirming the decline of the "trader" is a scan of job openings in the forex field. There is a preponderance of references to coding skills and financial engineering experience (see https://www.efinancialcareers.com/jobs-Trading.s035).

As artificial intelligence improves, the percentage of nonhuman trading will significantly increase. Humans trading will become an extinct species. Interestingly enough, following the economics of scarcity, as human traders get replaced, the few remaining will be more valuable than ever. Ultimately, however, just as in other fields, the future will feature a human collaborating with an AI-based system (or the AI system collaborating with a human!). This inevitability underscores the value of fundamental analysis. The human factor will add value to trading because it will bring to the decisions a human assessment of the fundamental forces. A key weakness in synthetic traders is that they cannot effectively evaluate real-time geopolitical events, and related shocks. Until algorithmic-based trading programs incorporate real-time detection of market emotions, they will be fatally limited. There is likely to be a role for the human factor, at least until there is the "singularity." Yet, until then, progress is being made. Let us explore the world of nonhuman-based assisted trading.

In fact, it is already happening. There are several types of primitive computer-assisted trading.

Bots

These are automatic trading systems that are based on algorithms (a set of rules) to convert data into information that leads to trading signals. They do the trading for the trader through EAs (expert assistants) that are linked to accounts, or coding using FIXED language. These types of bots are not really smart. A Tesla self-driving vehicle, or Google car can make mistakes in crossing the intersection, but they can learn from their mistakes. Bots, at the current level of design, do not learn from their mistakes. Bots are also essentially watching the price action only. They are very popular as traders are usually very lazy in trying to learn how to improve their trading. There is an every growing supply of bots because as a product, they are easy to sell. They also have an additional major flaw in that they do NOT use fundamental analysis as a reference for their rules.

Alerts

Alerts impact the traders frame of attention. An alert monitors a price action and is then programmed to provide a signal when a change has occurred. These are automatic alerts that communicate to the trader. For example, a system that scans all currency pairs and detects and alerts when any of them have probed or broken a 61.8% fib line would be useful to a trader who uses fib-based trading set-ups. The problem of price-based alerts is that there can be so many of them that they do not add value to the trader and might in fact be counterproductive.

Digital Trader Assistance: On-Demand Alerts

Consider a conversation that is likely to happen in the near future:

Trader: "Alexa, find FXDeepMind and tell me the condition of the EURUSD?"
Alexa: "The EURUSD is now @117.45. It is bullish in direction; the EURUSD is now number 1 in momentum leaderboard. Look to buy."
Trader: "Alexa, find Guru, and what is the latest on gold?"
Alexa: "Our gold expert, Mr. X, says gold is a long-term short as interest rates are likely to increase."

In the past, finding for a taxi required waiting for one to go through the intersection where one was waiting, or to specifically call for one and hope to get through. The era of on-demand service, let us call it the "uberization" of service delivery, will generate a new class of alerts. On demand alerts where the trader asks the "computer" for a specific answer on a currency pair's behavior. It is already here. The ability to "talk" to a digital assistant and obtain on-demand information will revolutionize a trader's ability to navigate through global markets.

FXDeepMind, developed by this author, is a unique program that embeds in Alexa the ability to monitor market conditions and also determine whether those conditions are bullish or bearish and the degree of bullish and bearishness. FXDeepMind is not limited to price action, but can access a variety of databases that offer sentiment and fundamental-based analysis to convert into a market conditions alert.

The emergence of the digital trader assistant via Google, Amazon, and other internet media will make the careers of brokers and trader advisors who are screen watchers obsolete as their methods become vastly inferior to the power of the embedded digital trading assistant such as FXDeepMind. In the near future, digital assistance will be able to place the trade as well.

* * *

Social Trading Alerts

Social trading has emerged as a form of trading assistance. Many websites offer lists of traders to copy. Their performance is also shown. A customer can choose to copy the trades of anyone on the leaderboard. This approach opens up new sources of signals. It also offers several challenges to the customer. First, there is not enough information regarding each trade. Knowing a trader's total performance is not enough. The leader in a list of traders might be in a performance vector that is declining, while a much less profitable trader could be in a performance sequence that is gaining. This level of information is not available.

Deep Learning Algorithms

Ultimately, forex trading will follow the path that is already happening with the use of AI in other fields. For example, in chess, computers provide huge assistance to world class players in identifying weaknesses in their opponent's history of moves. Humanity has, after being defeated in chess by the supercomputers, welcomed their assistance.

Gary Kasparov, the great world chess champion has written. "We are fantastic at teaching our machines how to do our tasks, and we will only get better at it." (*Deep Thinking*, Gary Kasparov, p. 258.)

In medicine, artificial intelligence is being used to provide diagnostic advice. When combined with human experts, the error rates are reported to be enormously decreased. The following quote applies to algorithms emerging in trading markets.

"The word 'diagnosis' comes from the Greek for 'knowing apart.' Machine-learning algorithms will only become better at such knowing apart—at partitioning, at distinguishing moles from melanomas. But knowing in all its dimensions transcends those task-focused algorithms. In the realm of medicine, perhaps the ultimate rewards come from knowing together." (The Algorithm Will See You Now, article in *New Yorker*, April 3, 2017.)

It is not surprising that AI has been making great strides, in areas such as medicine, because huge data mining has to occur, and the number of variables is known. In the markets, we have a problem similar to predicting when a hurricane will form. It is called irreducible complexity. We do not even know if we are missing variables. So AI programs for trading will add value, not detecting market behavior and patterns that are obscured by the market noise. One such program is called "Enigma Signal" (Enigmasignal.com). Its creator, Mark Sear, is a leader in big data and predictive analytics. The Enigma Signal charts using "swarm intelligence" to visualize the buying and selling patterns of large positions as dark swarms. These represent big corporate trades. Positions that represent

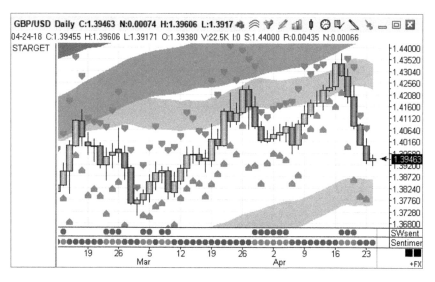

Chart 8.1 Artificial intelligence signals

more risk capital of intraday traders are shown as gray swarms. Furthermore, a deep learning program scans sentiment data (twitter feeds, text mining, etc.) and signals red, green, and gray conveying sentiment conditions when the market is persistently bullish, (green), bearish (red) and indecisive (gray). This AI application, when combined with good risk management, can be the next wave in improving a trader's path to profitability (Chart 8.1).

The most promising skill set that humans can bring to trading in this age of the emergence of AI is experiential knowledge that comes from trading. By trading, the trader develops a personal knowledge base of patterns that work and those that do not. The future of forex trading will be a partnership with our AI companions.

Conclusion

While one does not learn to trade from a book, it remains true that the winning trade begins before it is even taken. The attitudes and mind-set of the trader provide an analytical lens and a mental narrative which lead to the decisions to trade. In this context, the goal of Planet Forex has been to provide a new analytical vantage point for the currency trader.

Therefore, there are some conclusions about trading forex that should be highlighted.

1. Fundamental forces shape price action, but through sentiment.
2. Currency pairs' encode a balance of expectations about growth, interest rate decisions, and geopolitical risk.
3. Traditional reliance on technical analysis to shape a trade is deeply flawed without attention to the alignment of sentiment.
4. Three-line and Renko charting provide a level of granularity that clarifies the dominant sentiment prevailing in the market.

There is no substitute for putting on trades to experience and test new strategies. To that end, special coaching is available at www.learn4x.com on applying sentiment analysis to currency trading.

Best Wishes for Success in Trading.

Abe Cofnas

© The Author(s) 2018

A. Cofnas, *Planet Forex*, https://doi.org/10.1007/978-3-319-92913-2

Appendix: Resources for Sentiment Trading and Training

Readers of Planet Forex are welcome to explore the following sites for further contact with author Abe Cofnas:

1. WWW.LEARN4X.COM is the site owned by Abe Cofnas, author of Planet Forex and provides access to opportunities for private coaching on trading the strategies and tactics described in Planet Forex. Special sentiment alignment charting is provided with collaboration with Smarttick.com and MetaStock.com
2. EnigmaSignal.com is the site for the AI based charting using Swarm science and sentiment analysis. For further information on AI and sentiment analysis, Mr. Cofnas can be contacted at: tradercoach@enigmasignal.com
3. Customized charts and Private Coaching on Sentiment Trading techniques by Abe Cofnas is available. Mr. Cofnas can be contacted at skype id:learn4x and at abecofnas@gmail.com

© The Author(s) 2018
A. Cofnas, *Planet Forex*, https://doi.org/10.1007/978-3-319-92913-2

Index

© The Author(s) 2018
A. Cofnas, *Planet Forex*, https://doi.org/10.1007/978-3-319-92913-2